LEONARD A. STEVENS began writing adventure stories and science articles for *Collier's* magazine nearly twenty years ago. Subsequently, he has written scores of articles for various magazines, as well as over twenty books. Two of them, *SALUTE!* and *EQUAL!*, are part of Coward, McCann and Geoghegan's *Great Constitutional Issues* series.

Mr. Stevens was born in Lisbon, New Hampshire. He holds a BA and an MA from the University of Iowa, where his major was journalism. Mr. Stevens is deeply involved in civic affairs and environmental protection in his hometown, Bridgewater, Connecticut.

About the Book

On May 23, 1957, a cold, rainy day in Cleveland, Ohio, police without a search warrant broke into the home of Dollree Mapp, a young black women suspected of involvement in the city's gambling rackets. When she resisted the search of her home, Ms. Mapp was handcuffed while officers went through every room, rummaging through her bedroom drawers, closet, and suitcases. Bent on finding something which would allow them to arrest her, police finally seized upon some pornographic books, drawings, and photographs.

What then began as a "dirty little smut case" was to lead to one of this century's most important and controversial Supreme Court decisions.

With *TRESPASS!*, the author of *SALUTE!* and *EQUAL!* turns his attention to the case of *Mapp v. Ohio*, in which the fundamental right of a person to be secure in his home is at stake. What the Fourth Amendment to the U.S. Constitution says and what has been done in practice is the basis of an eye-opening and timely book that will be of interest to everyone who believes that a government should obey its own laws.

TRESPASS!

The People's Privacy vs.
the Power of the Police

Great Constitutional Issues:
The Fourth Amendment

by Leonard A. Stevens

CONSULTANTS:
John Lowenthal, Rutgers Law School
Louis H. Pollak,
University of Pennsylvania

Coward, McCann & Geoghegan, Inc.
New York

Copyright © 1977 by Leonard A. Stevens
All rights reserved. This book, or parts thereof, may not be
reproduced in any form without permission in writing from
the publisher. Published simultaneously in Canada by
Longman Canada Limited, Toronto.

Library of Congress Cataloging in Publication Data

Stevens, Leonard A
  Trespass!: The people's privacy vs. the power of the police.
  (Great constitutional issues: The Fourth amendment)
  Bibliography: p.
  Includes index.
  1. Mapp, Dollree.   I.   Title.
KF224.M28S7   345'.73'056   76-58018

SBN: 698-30663-5 lib. bdg.

Printed in the United States of America

TRESPASS!

Contents

Foreword

This book is the third in which Leonard A. Stevens has inquired in depth into a major Supreme Court decision that has breathed new life into one of the great liberties proclaimed in the Constitution. In *SALUTE!*, Stevens told the story of *Board of Education v. Barnette* (1943), the remarkable decision in which the Court, in the middle of World War II, vindicated the freedom of Americans to embrace unpopular religious and political views by sustaining the right of Jehovah's Witness children to refrain from saluting the flag in a public school classroom. In *EQUAL!*, Stevens advanced a decade to examine *Brown v. Board of Education* (1954), in which the Court, by striking down racial segregation in public schools, finally demonstrated that all Americans are created equal. This third volume moves ahead another decade to consider a case, *Mapp v. Ohio* (1961). By preventing state courts from accepting evidence of crime seized by police in an unlawful search, *Mapp* strengthened the right of every American to be free from lawless official intrusion upon the privacy of one's home and one's person.

9

Board of Education v. Barnette deals with the First Amendment's freedoms of worship and speech. *Brown v. Board of Education* is an application of the Fourteenth Amendment's promise of "equal protection of the laws." *Mapp v. Ohio* is rooted in the Fourth Amendment's ban on "unreasonable searches and seizures." The Fourth Amendment—like the First— was a part of the Bill of Rights, added to the Constitution in 1791 only two years after the Constitution went into force. The Fourth Amendment was adopted to prevent the officials of the newly independent American republic from engaging in the petty despotisms all too frequently indulged in by British officials before the American Revolution. Some ninety years ago, in one of its first extended inquiries into the genesis of the Fourth Amendment, the Supreme Court had this to say:

In order to ascertain the nature of the proceedings intended by the Fourth Amendment to the Constitution under the terms "unreasonable searches and seizures," it is only necessary to recall the contemporary or then recent history of the controversies on the subject, both in this country and in England. The practice had obtained in the Colonies, of issuing writs of assistance to the revenue officers, empowering them, in their discretion, to search suspected places for smuggled goods, which James Otis pronounced "the worst instrument of arbitrary power, the most destructive of English liberty and the fundamental principles of law, that ever was found in an English law book"; since they placed "the liberty of every man in the hands of every petty officer." This was in February, 1761, in Boston, and the famous debate in which it occurred was perhaps the most prominent event which inaugurated the resistance of the colonies to the oppressions of the mother country. "Then and there," said John Adams, "then and there was the first scene of the first act of opposition to the arbitrary claims of Great Britain. Then and there the child of Independence was born."

Dollree Mapp, whose trials and tribulations Stevens describes in this volume, might not appear to be a likely standard-bearer for the liberties espoused by James Otis and John Adams. Mapp, a black woman, was living precariously on the margins of the law. The case that brought her notoriety, and which enlarged the Constitution, began when Cleveland police came to her door waving a piece of paper they claimed to be a search warrant. When her case finally reached the Supreme Court of the United States, the question that the Court dealt with was whether a state's law enforcement officers could invade a home without legal authority and then build a criminal prosecution on evidence acquired through that lawless behavior. In answering that question, the Court undertook to strengthen constitutional provisions which, as the Court had said many years before, "apply to all invasions on the part of the government and its employes of the sanctity of a man's home and the privacies of life. It is not the breaking of his doors, and the rummaging of his drawers, that constitutes the essence of the offense; but it is the invasion of his indefeasible right of personal security, personal liberty and private property."

These were the liberties at stake in Ohio's attempt to imprison one of its citizens. In the pages that follow, Leonard Stevens presents in thoughtful and comprehensive detail the way in which Dollree Mapp's unprepossessing life became part of the living Constitution.

JOHN LOWENTHAL
Rutgers Law School
LOUIS H. POLLAK
University of Pennsylvania Law School

TRESPASS!

1

A Search and Seizure on Milverton Road

Early on the morning of May 23, 1957, a cold, rainy day in Cleveland, Ohio, police Sergeant Carl Delau received a telephone call at his home from Donald King, a local gambling figure, stating that someone had bombed his porch during the night. King, who was to become nationally prominent in the 1970s as a flamboyant promoter of international boxing matches involving the famous Muhammad Ali and other top fighters, was well known to Delau. The sergeant worked in the police department's Bureau of Special Investigations and had been dealing with the Cleveland gambling underworld for a long time. He knew it was a rough society laced with bitter rivalries and that King was part of it. In this realm, an occasional porch bombing was not unusual. So Delau was hardly surprised by King's complaint, and he promised to look into the matter.

Later that morning in downtown Cleveland Delau received an anonymous call declaring that if he went to 14705 Milverton Road in the Shaker Heights section of Cleveland he might find someone who knew about the bombing. Furthermore, said the nameless caller, Delau might also find a lot of "policy paraphernalia" (equipment and paperwork associated with an illegal form of gambling).

"Whose place is that?" asked Delau, trying to engage the caller in conversation to probe for more information.

"Dolly Mapp," replied the informer—and he hung up.

Dollree Mapp was a black woman in her late twenties whose fine features had sometimes led people to compare her with the lovely singer Lena Horne. She had come to Cleveland from Texas as a child to live with an aunt. As a young woman she had married a Cleveland boxer, Jimmy Bivens, but now, in 1957, they were divorced. More recently she had been known as a friend of Archie Moore, then the world's light heavyweight boxing champion.

Delau knew Dollree Mapp, and thought that she was somehow involved with the city's gambling rackets. However, to his knowledge she had never had any serious run-ins with the law.

After the anonymous call the sergeant decided to investigate the tip by visiting 14705 Milverton Road. Taking a car with two uniformed patrolmen, Michael Haney and Thomas Dever, Delau, a plainclothesman, drove out Kinsman Road to Shaker Heights, turned left on 147th Street, and proceeded to where it dead-ended with Milverton Road. From that intersection the address the policeman wanted was almost directly ahead, across from the end of 147th Street. It was a small, two-story brick house bordered by a narrow lawn and a driveway at the left leading to a garage. Actually it

16

was a two-family home with downstairs and upstairs apartments.

At the moment, late in the noon hour, Dollree Mapp, the owner of the house, was in the upstairs apartment where she lived with a teenage stepdaughter, Barbara Bivens, who was then at school for the day. Part of the downstairs apartment was rented to a friend, Minerva Tate, who was there at the time with a visitor, Virgil Ogletree.

The police turned off 147th Street on to Milverton and parked, directly across from the brick house. As the black and white vehicle pulled up to the curb, Ms. Mapp saw it from an upstairs window.

Delau and the two patrolmen got out and crossed the street to the house to check its two doors, one in front and one on the side by the driveway. They quickly concluded the side door, with Dollree Mapp's name on it, was the one they wanted, and the sergeant rang the bell.

"What do you want?" said a woman's voice from a second-story window which she had just opened. Delau recognized Dollree Mapp.

"Good afternoon, Dolly," he replied in a friendly manner, as if they had been old friends. "Oh, we just want to come in and take a look around."

"What for?" asked the owner, leaning across the windowsill.

Delau didn't answer directly. With only the anonymous tip to go by, he wasn't really sure what or whom he was hoping to find inside, so he purposely remained unclear about the visit. However, he kept insisting that he wanted to be let in. At the same time Ms. Mapp continued to press for the reason. She

17

suspected the policemen might be looking for Ogletree, the visitor downstairs, but as her questions
remained unanswered, she became more and more
determined not to let them in. She soon broke off the
conversation by closing the window.

Delau, twenty-seven years old, six feet two and 180
pounds, was incensed by the woman's refusal to open
up. He kept ringing the bell and knocking on the side
door, which led to the stairs and Ms. Mapp's
apartment. For a while there was no response.

In the meantime Ms. Mapp, increasingly upset by
the pounding on the door and the ringing of the bell,
called her attorney in downtown Cleveland. She had
recently retained a lawyer, A. L. Kearns, to bring a civil
damage suit against Archie Moore and the case was now
before the courts.

"Mr. Kearns is away today," explained a secretary.

"I need advice in a hurry," said Ms. Mapp.

"Mr. Greene, one of his partners, is here. Would you
care to speak with him?"

Ms. Mapp agreed and she was switched to Walter L.
Greene, a young man who had been out of law school
only a few years. He had joined the firm where his
father, Irwin Greene, had been Kearn's partner for
some time. "Do they have a search warrant?" asked the
young attorney.

"They didn't say so," replied Ms. Mapp.

"Well, you tell 'em that your lawyer says they can't
come in until they have a warrant. When they get one
properly drawn up, tell 'em they can come in."

In issuing the advice, the young lawyer was guided
by a false assumption that most Americans would have
followed in those days. He assumed that policemen

18

seldom searched a home without a search warrant properly filled out and approved by a judge in a court.* Actually, in practice it seldom happened. In this respect Delau was typical. He had conducted hundreds of searches around Cleveland without warrants. He believed, he says, that "Ohio law" didn't require such warrants.

The law behind Greene's assumption was mainly constitutional. The Constitution of the United States supposedly protects people against "unreasonable searches and seizures" of their "persons, houses, papers and effects," and it provides that searches are to be made only with warrants issued by a judge with good reason and "describing the place to be searched, and the persons or things to be seized." The Constitution of the State of Ohio contained similar provisions. However, in those days neither of the constitutional restraints appeared to have much effect on most policemen and other public officials.

But at the moment Greene's advice seemed to work. When Dollree Mapp opened her window and demanded that Delau produce a warrant, the policemen conferred for a moment, returned to their car, and drove away.

Ms. Mapp watched as the cruiser moved slowly down Milverton Road and disappeared. She then phoned Greene and reported on the results of his counsel.

"You may never see them again," the lawyer

*A warrant, or "writ," is a legal document issued by a judge giving an officer of the law the right to make an arrest, a search for, or a seizure of evidence in behalf of administering justice. When an officer is made to obtain a warrant, he is forced to allow a court to decide whether his proposed actions are truly in behalf of justice.

speculated. "Getting a search warrant may be more trouble than they feel the search is worth."

Agreeing to call him back if the police should return, Ms. Mapp hung up the phone and went back to the window. At first she saw nothing unusual, but then was startled when she caught sight of the police car parked on 147th Street about a block up from the intersection with Milverton. The police had just partly circled the block after leaving the front of the house. The two uniformed patrolmen were standing outside the car, and it appeared that Sergeant Delau was inside at the wheel.

"They think they're out of my sight," Ms. Mapp said to herself. "What could they be doing?" The car remained there for some time.

According to Delau, he had radioed back to headquarters and requested that a search warrant be obtained and delivered to him as soon as possible. It took time for it to be processed, the sergeant claimed, and he, Haney, and Dever were waiting patiently for the document to be delivered.

In that same period of time Ms. Mapp talked considerably with her downstairs tenant, Minerva Tate, and the visitor, Virgil Ogletree. Ms. Mapp later claimed that they felt the police were actually looking for Ogletree, but she, according to her recollections, was not about to let them into her house without a valid warrant, regardless of whether or not the tenant's visitor was implicated in some crime.

According to Delau, the processing and delivery of the search warrant took about two hours. It was delivered to him, he said, about four that afternoon, and it arrived with a lot of additional manpower. Delau and his two patrolmen were joined by several other police officers and their vehicles. The arrivals included a police lieutenant who, according to Patrolman Haney, brought the search warrant; an inspector; and two more local patrolmen who came in their radio cruisers. The small armada of police vehicles also included a black maria, a patrol wagon for transporting prisoners. They met on 147th Street and then moved slowly around to Milverton Road in front of the Mapp house.

During the afternoon, Dollree Mapp called attorney Greene at least twice more and reported on what she saw from the window. Around 3:15 Greene, after consulting his father, decided to go to the Mapp house. Carrying a 35 millimeter camera, he drove out to Shaker Heights and around to Milverton Road, arriving shortly after the large police force had gathered there.

"It was something out of the movies or TV," said the attorney. "There were the black and whites [patrol cars] with their flashing lights and cops all around. Neighbors from all up and down the street had gathered on the sidewalk across from Dolly Mapp's house, curious about what was happening."

Greene parked and, with his camera in hand, started for his client's house. But he had only walked a few yards when a uniformed policeman rushed his way, calling to the other officers to join him. Actually, the policeman had mistaken Greene for the nephew of a well-known Cleveland gambling figure, Shondor Birns, who in later years was to die when his car was bombed. The young attorney identified himself, the police recognized their error and allowed him to proceed toward the side door of the Mapp house

21

where, at the moment, Sergeant Delau was trying to force open the door.

Now Greene made a mistake in identity. He thought Delau was a judge he had recently seen in a local court. "Judge, what are you doing here?" the attorney asked.

Delau turned around and announced, incredulously, that he was not a judge, but a special investigator of the Cleveland police. He went back to work on the door as Greene, introducing himself as Ms. Mapp's attorney, protested.

"You don't have to do that!" Greene said. "If you have a search warrant, I'll see to it that you can go in."

Delau, as Greene remembers, wasn't interested. "We've been here two or three hours," the sergeant replied. "We're not going to fool around anymore."

The attorney, shaken by this rebuff, then decided the best he could do was to become a good witness to the break-in. He stepped back and, with his hands shaking, tried to adjust his lense to photograph Delau's activities, but he was so nervous that he dropped his camera on the wet lawn. Hurriedly cleaning off the case, the now embarrassed attorney began shooting pictures from hip level, not even sighting through the viewfinder.

If the pictures had come out well, which they didn't, they might have shown Delau going through the door. Dollree Mapp, who was just descending the stairs on the inside, claims the sergeant had broken the glass, reached in, and released the lock.

Delau, followed by several uniformed policemen, rushed through the door and up the stairs. Greene moved in behind the last of them, a tall, heavy inspector wearing a blue rain cape. According to the attorney the inspector suddenly whirled, his cape flying open, and there in the man's hand was a pistol pointing directly at the lawyer, who promptly withdrew.

As Delau rushed up the stairs, Dollree Mapp demanded to see a search warrant. The sergeant held up and waved a paper on which there was typewriting. He didn't intend to give it to her, but Ms. Mapp reached forward, snatched it out of his hand, and stuffed the document down the front of her dress, depositing it in her bosom.

According to Ms. Mapp, one of the policemen on the stairs, probably Haney, yelled, "Wow! She's got it in her bosom. What do we do now?"

"Go after it!" she recalls Delau replying loudly.

A scuffle ensued as the police tried to wrestle free the paper, and Ms. Mapp slapped and scratched at their faces. During that encounter, she remembers that her fingernails cut into one or more of the policemen and they in turn cursed her out as a "black nigger bitch!"

When the fracas was over, Dollree Mapp no longer had the paper, but was in handcuffs and being led back upstairs, to a room where, she recalls, a patrolman guarded her while the others began a wide-ranging search of the house. The police simultaneously entered the downstairs apartment, which was open to the stairway and the broken side door. They immediately found Virgil Ogletree and arrested him as a suspect involved with the bombing of Donald King's house.

As Ogletree was led from the house and placed in the black maria, Greene finally adjusted his camera properly and photographed the event. In his Cleveland office he still has a brownish, fading snapshot of

Ogletree, a black man in a long topcoat, being guided into a police patrol wagon.

It's safe to guess that if Dollree Mapp had not resisted the search of her house early that afternoon, Ogletree would have been arrested and Delau, Haney, and Dever might have left satisfied. But as it was Ms. Mapp's resistance apparently infuriated the police, aroused their suspicions, or both, to the point where they were bent on finding something which would also allow them to arrest her.

They literally went through the house from top to bottom. While Dollree Mapp sat in handcuffs and was guarded by a patrolman, the other officers searched every room in her apartment. They rummaged through her bedroom drawers, closet, and suitcases. They searched the kitchen and the living room. And they went through her stepdaughter's bedroom. Other officers covered the downstairs apartment and even the basement where they searched through boxes and suitcases stored there. At one point Ms. Mapp was led to the stairs where she was handcuffed to a banister rung while her guard joined the search.

When they were done, the police had a large collection of items with which Delau believed he could bring charges against the owner of the house. First they had a box of lottery slips which he felt could serve as evidence to bring a charge for possession of "policy paraphernalia." This would be considered only a misdemeanor, not a very serious offense, but in the remaining loot he felt there were items that could be the basis of an extremely serious charge. They were, as identified by the police, obscene books, drawings, and photographs involving human sexual acts. At the time a tough Ohio law made it a felony (a grave crime) for a person simply to possess obscene materials. The penalty could be a $2,000 fine or seven years in prison, or both.

As Ms. Mapp remained handcuffed to the banister, she recalls that the police assembled in the hallway and inspected their findings. They were particularly interested in four books, she claims, and appeared to go through every page. "They seemed to enjoy them immensely," says Ms. Mapp.

"They don't belong to me," she claims to have told the police that afternoon. "They belong to Morris Jones, who rented a room from me. They were in his things that I'm keeping for him while he's away."

Her protest was ignored, and she was placed under arrest. Releasing her from the stairway, the officers told Ms. Mapp to put on her coat, for she was going to the police court. They soon led her outside to one of the police cars, put her in the back seat, and the police entourage drove away followed by attorney Greene. The neighbors, still puzzled by the arrests, returned to their homes, and Milverton Road settled back to its quiet, relatively boring suburban atmosphere.

None of the principals or observers of this ordinarily routine police action had any way of knowing it, but the home of Dollree Mapp had been subject to one of the most famous, or infamous, searches and seizures in the history of the United States. What was starting that day as a dirty little "smut case" was to lead to one of the century's most important and controversial decisions of the Supreme Court of the United States.

The case of *Mapp v. Ohio,** which had just begun,

*v. (for *Versus*) means "against" in Latin.

would go to the heart of a fundamental issue of freedom in America, indeed, an issue that had led directly to the American Revolution.

2

The Freedom of One's House

As Sergeant Carl Delau escorted Dollree Mapp from her Cleveland home in May 1957, they were on the way to playing a key role in a vital concept of human freedom that has been an issue for centuries. It involves the fundamental right of a person to be secure and private in his home, a right that should not be violated except for lawful reasons clearly related to the common good of all people. In the most lawful instances violations of this basic right have been associated with "searches and seizures" where public officials, in the administration of justice, have been looking for evidence or individuals related to a crime. The most unlawful violations have been "searches and seizures" conducted with no reason except to harass an individual, to pry needlessly into his private life, or simply on the chance of finding something to use against the person.

The concept of a person's right to be private and secure in his home was embodied in Biblical law, which forbade entering a person's home without proper permission. The principle of the home being sacred was found in Roman history, where the great orator Cicero declared, "What is more inviolable, what better defended by religion than the house of a citizen? . . . This place of refuge is so sacred to all men that to be dragged from thence is unlawful."

Foundations for the legal principles of search and seizure in the United States were put down in early English law. Some of them were indicated by the Magna Carta, the most important document of English constitutional history, issued in 1215 by King John. English legislation on the issue of search and seizure began early in the following century.

But the British history of the subject has many chapters of abuses condoned by English monarchs against citizens. In the 1500s and 1600s the infamous Court of Star Chamber authorized blanket searches without reasons, and they established precedents under which British citizens and subjects suffered far into the future. Growing opposition to these practices in the eighteenth century led to debates before the British Parliament. From them came one of history's most eloquent statements on the principle that a person's home should be as safe for him as a castle for a king. It was delivered by William Pitt, the first Earl of Chatham, who proclaimed:

"The poorest man may, in his cottage, bid defiance to all the forces of the crown. It may be frail; its roof may shake; the wind may blow through it; the storm may enter; but the King of England may not enter; all his force dares not cross the threshold of the ruined tenement."

One of the most important trials in American history involved a case of unreasonable search and seizure imposed upon the British colonies in the 1750s and 1760s. It was brought to the Superior Court of the province of Massachusetts Bay in 1761 by sixty-three Boston merchants who were contesting an insidious form of search warrant known as the "writs of assistance." The writs, which had been issued to custom inspectors, amounted to open-ended licenses from the English government allowing the officers to search anywhere for "uncustomed" goods (goods smuggled into the colonies to avoid customs fees).

In fact, a writ of assistance was more than a license for the holder to search. It literally commanded all officers and subjects of the Crown to help him search. Thus the holder of a writ could demand and expect help from anyone in carrying out his mission. Furthermore, the man with a writ didn't have to explain himself when he launched a search. He could enter a house or any place at will and search every cranny and every object without fear of legal repercussion.

Once an official had been issued a writ, it was his to use indefinitely, search after search. And, indeed, a writ holder was motivated to search as much as possible because the government gave him a one-third share of the uncustomed goods he found and possessed. This led rapacious custom officials to trespass, cause or no cause, and they often profiteered from their booty.

The writs of assistance turned one Charles Paxton into the most unpopular man in Boston. He was the surveyor of customs of the Port of Boston, a man who used his unbridled power of search with great vigor. He eventually became the defendant in a lawsuit brought by the legislature of the province accusing him of illegally dipping into the government's share of seized

29

merchandise. He nearly lost the case, but was saved by a legal technicality; nevertheless, the case revealed how the man was profiteering from his unlimited power to search and seize, and it made his fellow Bostonians dislike him more than ever.

The controversy over Paxton and the writs of assistance came to a head in 1761, six months after the death of King George II, when by English law all writs expired. Paxton applied for a reissuance of the infamous warrants, and the sixty-three Boston merchants appealed to the Superior Court to discontinue the despised practice.

The merchants' case was carried by two attorneys, James Otis, Jr., and Oxenbridge Thacher. The custom officers were represented by Jeremiah Gridley, attorney general of Massachusetts Bay. Both he and Thacher presented highly competent, technical arguments for and against the use of the writs of assistance in America, but it was Otis, known as Boston's most competent attorney, who went to the heart of the writs themselves, damning their very existence in a free society. The attorney denounced unreasonable search and seizure as ". . . a power that places the liberty of every man in the hands of every petty officer." His carefully framed oration, lasting four to five hours, won him an enduring place in the history books of America:

> Now, one of the most essential branches of English liberty is the freedom of one's house. A man's house is his castle; and whilst he is quiet, he is as well guarded as a prince in his castle. The writ, if it should be declared legal, would totally annihilate this privilege. Customhouse officers

may enter our houses when they please; we are commanded to permit their entry. Their menial servants may enter, may break locks, bars and everything in their way; and whether they break through malice or revenge, no man, no court, can inquire. Bare suspicion without oath is sufficient. This wanton exercise of this power is not a chimerical [absurd] suggestion of a heated brain. . . . What a scene does this open! Every man, prompted by revenge, ill humor, or wantonness to inspect the inside of his neighbor's house, may get a writ of assistance. Others will ask [for the same] from self-defense; one arbitrary exertion will provoke another, until society be involved in tumult and blood.

Despite Otis's powerful challenge of the writs, the justices who heard him were not impressed enough to act promptly against the warrants. But the words spoken by Otis found their mark with others whose actions would be far more significant than the decision the court would render.

In the audience as Otis spoke was the twenty-five-year-old John Adams, who was to become a patriot leader in the American Revolution and the second President of the United States. The speech against the writs of assistance had a powerful impact on the young man, and through Adams and others the words of James Otis helped kindle resistance to British rule in America.

"I do say in the most solemn manner," Adams wrote at a much later date, "that Mr. Otis's oration against the Writs of Assistance breathed into this nation the breath

31

of life. [He] was a flame of fire! Every man of a crowded audience appeared to me to go away, as I did, ready to take arms against Writs of Assistance. Then and there was the first scene of opposition to the arbitrary claims of Great Britain. Then and there the child Independence was born. In 15 years, namely in 1776, he grew to manhood, and declared himself free."

While the Otis speech was also to be compared with the famous orations of Patrick Henry in Virginia, which helped move the South to revolt against the British, the Bostonian did not win the Boston merchants their day in court.

The five justices didn't act for ten months, and then, following another hearing, they decided to reissue the despised warrants. The first one went to Charles Paxton, the most disliked man in Boston.

The lost case of the writs remained a keystone of resistance up into the Revolutionary War, but then, as a constitution for the new government of the United States was framed in 1787, it failed to address the issue of search and seizure which had played such an important role in sparking the American Revolution. It was felt by many of the framers that protection from illegal search and seizure, as well as other civil liberties, was already provided by the states' constitutions, most of which had a "bill of rights" to safeguard the liberties of individuals. The lack of such measures in the new national Constitution became a cornerstone of opposition to the document by the "Anti-Federalists," who feared that it gave too much power to a strong central government. They feared the rights of individuals would soon be forgotten regardless of the

32

protections offered by state constitutions. This specter stirred memories of the writs of assistance and of what a king could do with unbridled powers of search and seizure.

When the new Constitution went to the thirteen states for ratification, after slipping through the national Congress it arrived in Virginia, where the leader of its opposition was the forceful Patrick Henry. He used his oratorical gifts to strike an emotional blow based on the old issue of search and seizure. He pointed out that there could very well be federal sheriffs in Virginia under superiors located far from the state. The sheriffs, he added, could very well be working with tax and revenue collectors. He continued, "When these harpies [the sheriffs] are aided by excisemen [the collectors], who may search, at any time, your houses and most secret recesses, will the people bear it? If you think so, you differ with me. . . ."

A few days later Virginia's orator—who had won lasting fame in 1775 with his cry for liberty or death—again denounced the Constitution for its failure to protect the people's rights to be private and secure in their homes without fear of federal agents. "The officers of Congress may come upon you now," Henry proclaimed, "fortified with all the terrors of paramount federal authority. Excisemen may come in multitudes; for the limitations of their numbers no man knows. They may, unless the [federal] government be restrained by a bill of rights, or some similar restriction, go into your cellars and rooms, and search, ransack, and measure everything you eat, drink, or wear. They ought to be restrained within proper bounds."

The lack of a bill of rights posed a serious threat to the chances for the Constitution's ratification by all thirteen states.

In the next few months eleven states ratified the Constitution, with five of the most important calling for amendments that could serve as a bill of rights. With Rhode Island and North Carolina yet to ratify the document, the federal government began functioning troubled by an air of uncertainty and fear arising from the dissension behind its newly born Constitution.

It was evident that the omission of a bill of rights required immediate attention, and George Washington, the first President under the Constitution, addressed the matter at the earliest possible moment of his administration; in fact, he did so in his inaugural address. The chief drafter and leading supporter of the Constitution, James Madison of Virginia, became the first sponsor of amendments setting forth a bill of rights. He had been elected to the First Congress with the previous understanding that he would call for the amendments. Only four days after Washington's inaugural Madison announced his intentions to move in favor of constitutional amendments to serve as a bill of rights. Shortly he advanced a series of proposals that were the basis for what soon became the Bill of Rights (the first ten amendments to the Constitution). One of Madison's proposals, after a few revisions in the new Congress, became the Fourth Amendment:

The right of the people to be secure in their persons, papers, and effects, against unreasonable

34

searches and seizures, shall not be violated and no Warrants shall issue, but upon probable cause, supported by oath or affirmation, and particularly describing the place to be searched, and the persons or things to be seized.

The Amendment, whose words remain intact today, simply declares that searches and seizures must be reasonable and that they should be permitted only through search warrants issued for good cause by a judge with particular reference to the place to be searched and the people or things to be seized. The Amendment has the purpose of protecting what a famous justice of the Supreme Court, Louis Brandeis, once called "the right to be let alone—the most comprehensive of rights and the right most valued by civilized men."

Despite its high purpose the Amendment failed to address the key question of how it would be enforced. Violators would be officers of the law, the policeman, the sheriff, and in modern times the FBI and CIA agent. How would they be penalized for trespassing? Would the policeman arrest himself? Could he be sued by the victim? The Fourth Amendment is mute on such questions.

These issues, indeed, remained unsettled for a century and three quarters. In the meantime, the Supreme Court of the United States acted upon several important search and seizure cases, but the justices failed to answer the question of what to do about official violators of the Fourth Amendment—that is, until the case of *Mapp v. Ohio* came to their attention.

3

Vendors of Plate Glass and Two Gamblers

The job of interpreting the Constitution falls to the Supreme Court as it decides various cases involving important constitutional issues. But this process didn't start for the Fourth Amendment until nearly a century after its ratification. During the first half of our history, federal criminal laws were few, and federal criminal cases were less common than today. Issues of search and seizure were not often tried. The first major Supreme Court case on search and seizure didn't occur until the 1880s.

In the autumn of 1882, when the Federal Building in Philadelphia was under construction, the government notified suppliers that it was accepting bids (price quotations) for a great deal of polished plate glass which would have to be imported from abroad. Edward A. and George H. Boyd of New York City filed their bid on the glass and won the contract. Because the federal government was buying the glass, it agreed that no custom fees would need to be paid to the United States and that customs collectors at the Port of New York would be so notified when the glass arrived.

37

Soon after the contract was signed, and well before the glass was due in New York, the architect for the Philadelphia building asked the Boyds if they could supply some three dozen cases of glass from stock they had previously received and paid customs upon. The Boyds agreed and shipped the glass with the understanding that they would be allowed to replace the stock with a like amount of glass imported free of customs charges.

A few months later Edward and George Boyd found themselves charged with fraud in the United States District Court for the Southern District of New York. As the case of *Boyd v. United States* went up to the Supreme Court, it established certain lasting points in the federal courts about search and seizure; moreover, it became a remarkable preview of the confusing history that would unfold for the Fourth Amendment in the following century. Though *Boyd* was a landmark case in search and seizure, it involved neither a search nor a seizure.

As the Boyds' stock of glass had been replaced with duty-free glass, the customs collector in New York decided the glass vendors had deceived the government into allowing them two duty-free shipments when they were supposed to receive only one. The first lot in question, twenty-nine cases, arrived from England on the steamer *Baltic*. The second of thirty-five cases came on the vessel *Alaska*. The government claimed that the Boyds had somehow manipulated paperwork and illegally avoided paying customs on the thirty-five cases. If true, this would have been a crime with severe penalties. The Boyds would not only have to forfeit the expensive glass itself, but they then could be sentenced to a fine of up to $5,000 and two years in jail.

During a jury trial in New York the glass vendors were ordered by the judge to bring in bills and other papers associated with the first shipment of glass. The papers were simply to be read in court and perhaps copied by the government attorneys, but the material was not to be taken away from the Boyds.

The accused and their attorney didn't like the order, but they complied, and the contents of the papers were put into evidence and used against the Boyds before a jury. It led to a verdict of guilty. The Boyds appealed to the next higher federal court, the circuit court of appeals, and again lost. Next they went to the Supreme Court of the United States, and they won, as the judgment of the circuit court was reversed.

Justice Joseph P. Bradley explained in the opinion of the Supreme Court that in forcing the Boyds to produce their papers as evidence their civil rights had been violated in two ways. First, the order amounted, in effect, to an unreasonable search and seizure of the papers. Thus the evidence used against the Boyds had been obtained illegally. For this, the opinion concluded, the Fourth Amendment was violated. Second, the order simultaneously violated a part of the Fifth Amendment which states that "No person . . . shall be compelled in any criminal case to be a witness against himself. . . ." The Boyds had been forced to bring their own damning evidence to court, Justice Bradley held, and thereby had been forced to become witnesses against themselves.

The Boyd decision established one of the most controversial rules in constitutional law. It was to become the key to the fate of Dollree Mapp, and her case was to heat up a debate over the rule that had continued for decades. It is known as the "exclusionary rule." When applied by a court it simply means that evidence obtained by illegal search and seizure cannot be used against someone in a trial. No matter how damaging illegally obtained evidence might be—even if it could clearly prove murder, kidnapping, the worst of crimes—the rule would prevent its use, even if it meant letting the criminal go free.

In the opinion of many authorities the exclusionary rule is the only way to punish police, public prosecutors, and other officials who violate the Fourth Amendment by failing to obtain properly drawn warrants. These authorities believe there is no other way to ensure that the Amendment will, in fact, protect citizens from illegal searches and seizures.

Consider the problem with a typical example. When policemen break into a person's home without a warrant, the question arises, how should the officer be punished for violating the law? The policeman isn't likely to turn himself in, nor are his superiors apt to prosecute the officer. The victim of the search might sue him for trespassing or burglary, but that's difficult and unlikely. So the answer usually comes back to the exclusionary rule. By its use courts thus notify police and others that warrantless, unreasonable searches and seizures will be a waste of time because the illegally obtained evidence will not be allowed in court.

One more important point about the exclusionary rule is that it is a rule developed by the courts. It is not statute law, that is, law passed by legislatures, such as

Congress. Nor is it found in the Constitution. The Fourth Amendment actually says nothing about how its violators should be punished. So the exclusionary rule, because of its creation by judges instead of legislators, has troubled some authorities who believe judges should not have taken it upon themselves to fashion a rule for enforcement of the Constitution not plainly recorded by the framers of the Constitution.

The exclusionary rule, which was established in our courts by the *Boyd* decision, was interpreted twice by the Supreme Court in the first fifteen years of the twentieth century, and the results left the Fourth Amendment somewhat two sided. The two cases that put the exclusionary rule to the test involved alleged gamblers Albert J. Adams of New York and Fremont Weeks of Kansas City.

One day soon after the turn of the century the New York police suspected that Albert Adams was involved in an illegal gambling game known as "policy." The game was a lottery in which players bought numbered tickets at various shops and either won or lost in a daily drawing held by the game's operators at their head-quarters. The police in the Adams case obtained a warrant allowing them to search his office for num-bered policy slips as evidence of his illegal gambling activity. When they arrived, Adams was out, but they entered anyway and immediately found a large pile of policy slips, some 3,500 of them. As the police continued the search, Adams arrived and was arrested. When their foray was over, the police left with Adams, the policy slips, and some of the arrested man's private papers which had not been mentioned in the search warrant. Eventually the papers were used in a trial as handwriting samples. They became important evidence for finding Adams guilty.

He was subject to a thousand-dollar fine and/or two years in jail, but Adams and his attorneys appealed his case from the New York courts all the way to the Supreme Court of the United States. Their appeal invoked the Fourth, Fifth, and Fourteenth Amendments to the Constitution, the Fourteenth having been adopted after the Civil War to prevent states from denying citizens (specifically the freed slaves) their rights under the Bill of Rights.

The attorneys claimed that in taking Adams' private papers, when the search warrant listed only the policy slips, the police had violated the Fourth Amendment. They reasoned that the private papers were illegally obtained and should not have been admitted in evidence by the judge in the trial against Adams.

Since his papers had been admitted, his lawyers argued, his Fifth Amendment rights had been violated. Adams had, in effect, been forced to testify against himself.

Finally, the lawyers argued that the Supreme Court should consider the Adams case under a part of the Fourteenth Amendment to the Constitution, which commands that no state shall "deprive any person of life, liberty or property without due process of law [proper legal proceedings]." New York, they contended, had so deprived their client by not allowing him the protection of the Fourth and Fifth Amendments of the Constitution of the United States.

The response to these pleas was found in the Supreme Court's opinion written by Justice William R.

Day. He did not deny that when Adams' papers were seized in violation of the Fourth Amendment they became illegal evidence, but he refused to agree that they should have been excluded from the trial. In support of this reasoning the High Court relied on an old rule of common law, the judge-made (and unwritten) law which, in our system of justice, was developed mostly in English courts of earlier times. Essentially, the rule said that the progress of a trial seeking the truth of a question should not be interrupted to argue over the legality of how this or that evidence was obtained. The New York court had followed the common-law rule in deciding the Adams case, and Justice Day and his brethren on the court felt it had plenty of precedent for doing so. As time would tell, the conflict between the exclusionary rule and common-law rule would continue to plague judges.

As to whether Adams' Fifth Amendment rights had been violated, the Supreme Court felt not. While the illegally obtained papers had been used against him, Justice Day declared, Adams had not been personally forced to testify about them on the witness stand. So that argument raised by the appellant's attorneys was rejected.

As to the question about the Fourteenth Amendment, the Court's opinion simply said, "We do not feel called upon to discuss [this] contention. . . ."

The judgment of the New York court was affirmed, and the loser, Albert Adams, went back for sentencing.

This Supreme Court decision established an important precedent for the exclusionary rule. It said that the Supreme Court of the United States would not force the rule on state courts. If they wanted to follow the common-law rule of not interrupting trials and thus allow illegally seized evidence to be used in court, that was their business. Put another way, the Supreme Court said that, at least as far as the exclusionary rule was concerned, the Fourth Amendment didn't necessarily apply to the states.

Fremont Weeks, the second alleged gambler to go to the Supreme Court with a search and seizure issue, appeared there ten years later and was victorious in a situation that seemed on the face of it comparable to that which left Adams a loser.

In 1911 Weeks was an employee of an express company in the Union Station at Kansas City, Missouri. The police of that city suspected he was using the mails to send out lottery tickets to gambling customers. Without a warrant of any kind, a policeman arrested Weeks at the railroad station while other officers went to his home to look for evidence proving he was violating a federal law. A neighbor revealed where Weeks hid a key to his house, and the police used it to enter and search the premises. They left with various papers and articles which they felt could be used against Weeks.

Later that day the police officers returned to the house with a United States marshal, and this time, after knocking on the door, were let in by a boarder who had just come home. Neither the police nor the marshal had a warrant, but they still proceeded to search Weeks' home thoroughly, and again numerous items were seized and removed. The booty, it turned out, included mining stock worth $12,000, insurance policies, currency totaling $75, candy, clothes, and a valuable newspaper published in 1790.

Before his trial in a federal court in Missouri, Weeks, represented by an attorney, petitioned to have the seized material returned to him. It was taken, he argued, in violation of the constitutions of Missouri and of the United States. When the court refused the request, certain letters were used as evidence in the trial, and Weeks was found guilty of illegally using the United States mails for gambling purposes.

When the case of *Weeks v. United States* arrived at the Supreme Court in December 1913, Weeks' attorney argued that his client's rights had been violated under both the Fourth and Fifth Amendments to the Constitution. The lawyer contended that both the Kansas City police and the United States marshal, acting without warrants, were guilty of an illegal search and seizure. Their loot, he maintained, should never have been admitted in evidence at the Weeks trial, but should have been returned as requested by the accused man.

On February 2, 1914, the Supreme Court handed down its decision with Justice Day again writing the opinion of the Court. This time he agreed that the illegally seized evidence should not have been admitted in evidence against the accused, but the justice did so only because of the violation of the Fourth Amendment committed by the United States marshal, an officer of the federal government.

We therefore reach the conclusion [stated Justice Day], that the letters in question were taken from the house of the accused by an official of the United States, acting under color of his office, in direct violation of the constitutional rights of the defendant [Weeks]; that having made a seasonable [advance] application for their return . . . the federal court in which Weeks was tried should have restored these letters to the accused.

In the same conclusion Justice Day went on, in effect, to excuse the Kansas City police for their part in the illegal search and seizure. "As to the papers and property seized by the policemen," the justice stated, "it does not appear that they acted under any claim of federal authority such as would make the [Fourth] amendment applicable to such unauthorized seizures. . . . What remedies the defendant may have against them we need not inquire, as the 4th Amendment is not directed to individual misconduct of such officials."

These few sentences were among the most important to be written about the Fourth Amendment in the twentieth century. They declared that the exclusionary rule applied only to federal police, such as United States marshals and (when it was formed) the FBI, but, as the *Adams* case established, it did not apply to state and local police. As it turned out, this meant that for nearly half a century state and local police could, in most cases, proceed in searches and seizures without fear of restrictions from the Fourth Amendment of the Constitution of the United States. Supreme Court Justice Hugo Black emphasized this many years later when he wrote:

Certainly there are far more state than federal enforcement officers and their activities up to now have more frequently and closely touched the intimate daily lives of people than have the activities of federal officers. A state officer's "knock at the door . . . as a prelude to a search, without authority of law," may be, as our experience shows, just as ominous to "ordered liberty" as though the knock were made by a federal officer.

4

When Searches Were Not Searches

When Sergeant Carl Delau of the Cleveland police went to the home of Dollree Mapp without a search warrant in 1957, he was following the rule and not the exception of police practices in America. For years in Cleveland recruits and other police officers were informed that the Constitution of Ohio forbade unreasonable searches and seizures, and they were told of the rules for conducting legal searches and seizures; however, the starch was quickly removed from such instructions when the recruits were assured that even if evidence were illegally seized, Ohio courts would allow it to be used in a trial. The Ohio Supreme Court had, indeed, made it clear that Ohio's lower courts were not to limit state law enforcement officers in the way the Supreme Court of the United States limited federal officers by fashioning the exclusionary rule.

This position, which was widely held throughout the United States, meant that search warrants were hardly used in many places, like Cleveland, where a great many searches and seizures were certain to occur. While schoolteachers and their pupils were assuming

49

that America lived by the maxim that a man's home is his castle and cannot be entered by officials high or low without a warrant, it simply was not true. Search warrants were practically unknown to the police of many American cities. In 1954, for example, Joseph Hadley, who had headed the city attorney's criminal division of Minneapolis since 1929, stated that he could remember only two search warrants being issued during his quarter century on the job. Later, in New York City the deputy police commissioner told the New York *Times* that "nobody bothered to take out search warrants."

While state and local law officers, and thus the majority of such officials in America, were acting for decades as though there were no Fourth Amendment, the Supreme Court of the United States devoted a great deal of time to the Amendment—although the majority of the justices continued supporting the *Weeks* decision that the exclusionary rule applied only to federal cases. Much of the time was consumed trying to define what was meant by the "unreasonable searches and seizures" referred to in the Amendment— but always the Court confined itself to cases involving federal officers. In some instances the decisions strengthened the Amendment, but in others its meaning was diluted and obscured.

In 1920, in a decision entitled *Silverthorne Lumber Company v. United States*, the Supreme Court strengthened the use of the exclusionary rule. Federal officers in this case had arrested officials of the lumber company and then searched their homes without a warrant. The officers took books, papers, and company records, which a court then ordered to be returned to the owner. The federal men did so, but kept photos and other copies of the material. Then these copies were used to obtain a court subpoena (a legal order) forcing the owners to return the originals to be used as evidence. The Supreme Court refused to accept such a roundabout procedure, saying that how the evidence was obtained in the first place was what counted. The evidence should have been permanently excluded from the court proceedings, said the High Court, because it had been illegally seized in a warrantless search.

In 1921 the Supreme Court considered a case in which two thieves had blown up two safes and forced open a desk to find papers that could be used against the owner. They turned the papers over to federal officers, who then introduced them in a trial against the owner. The Supreme Court allowed this unusual procedure to stand, explaining that the Fourth Amendment applied only to searches and seizures by government officials and not private citizens, like the thieves. Justice Louis D. Brandeis dissented to this decision, saying that "Respect for law will not be advanced by resort, in its enforcement, to means which shock the common man's sense of decency and fair play."

A little later the Court considered a case in which two federal officers hid themselves on the land of a man they suspected of selling whiskey in violation of the federal "prohibition" law which banned the manufacture and sale of alcoholic beverages. When they saw him step out of his house and pass a bottle of whiskey to another person, they seized the liquor and arrested the homeowner. They were trespassing on the man's land, but the question arose as to whether the evidence was obtained in violation of the Fourth Amendment. The Supreme Court said no, because there was actually no search of the "persons, houses, papers, and effects," the words used in the Amendment.

Of all the cases in which the Court defined searches and seizures, perhaps the most famous and difficult arrived from the state of Washington in 1928. It was a case that had arisen under the National Prohibition Act, and it involved an amazing conspiracy to violate the Act by "bootleggers" who were unlawfully importing, transporting, possessing, and selling intoxicating liquor. The general manager of the illegal business was Roy Olmstead.

To obtain evidence of what they suspected Olmstead was up to, four federal prohibition officers hired a telephone lineman to tap the wires of the suspect's offices, his home, and the homes of some of his colleagues. None of their properties was trespassed upon, for the taps were made in the basement of a large office building and in the streets near the homes. For many months the federal men listened and made stenographic notes of the conversations they heard. Eventually they assembled a picture of a huge, highly profitable business that was completely illegal under the prohibition law.

Olmstead, they found, had about fifty employees who were using two seagoing vessels to transport liquor into the state of Washington from nearby British Columbia. The liquor was stored in a large, underground hideout beyond the Seattle city limits. Several smaller secret storage spots were kept in the city.

The organization included a large central office with

telephone operators, executives, a sales staff, deliverymen, bookkeepers, bill collectors, and even an attorney. The wiretappers learned that this illegal business received about $176,000 a month in proceeds from sales of booze. It averaged about two hundred cases of liquor a day. Olmstead's initial investment was only $10,000, and eleven other investors had put up $1,000 each.

When their wiretap evidence was complete enough, the prohibition officers began arresting the bootleggers and their customers. In total seventy-five people were indicted (formally accused of the crime) and many were convicted in the federal district court in Washington state of breaking the Prohibition Act. Olmstead and two fellow conspirators, Charles S. Green and Edward H. McInnis, appealed to the Circuit Court of Appeals, lost, and then appealed to the Supreme Court of the United States. Their main contention was that their rights under the Fourth Amendment had been violated by the wiretaps. The tapping of their telephones, their attorneys argued, amounted to unreasonable searches and seizures by federal officers and the evidence thus acquired should not have been allowed in court.

A slim majority of the High Court ruled that wiretapping wasn't an unreasonable search and seizure. The majority opinion was written by Chief Justice William Howard Taft, who had served as the twenty-seventh President of the United States, from 1909 to 1913. He had been appointed chief justice in 1921.

He failed to see how the electronic seizure of a message from a telephone wire could be considered a search as set forth in the Fourth Amendment which, he said, declares a search "to be of material things—the person, the house, his papers, or his effects." The chief justice couldn't understand how a search warrant could be written for a wiretap because "it must specify the place to be searched and the person or *things* to be seized."

The Court had been urged to think of a wiretap in the same vein as opening a sealed letter and reading the content as it passed through the U.S. mails. A Supreme Court decision far back in 1877 had ruled that the opening of letters by a mail clerk was a search and seizure of the sender's papers or effects. But Chief Justice Taft couldn't see the analogy with an electrically conveyed message.

"The language of the [Fourth] amendment," he concluded, "cannot be extended and expanded to include telephone wires, reaching to the whole world from the defendant's house or office. The intervening wires are not part of his house or office, any more than are the highways along which they are stretched."

Oddly enough, the state of Washington had passed a law in 1909 making it a misdemeanor (a relatively minor crime) for anyone to "intercept, read or in any manner interrupt or delay the sending of a message over any telegraph or telephone line." This clearly meant that the evidence gathered by the federal wiretappers was illegally obtained, but Chief Justice Taft refused to say it should have been excluded from the Olmstead trial. In fact, he seemed to take the occasion to speak out against the exclusionary rule in general. He was clearly in favor of the old common-law rule of using evidence regardless of how obtained.

" . . . our general experience," he stated, "shows that

much evidence has always been receivable, although not obtained by conformity to the highest ethics."

This point and others were sharply contested in an eloquent dissent delivered by Justice Louis D. Brandeis. First he disagreed with restricting the words of the Fourth Amendment to their literal interpretation instead of looking to the principles behind the words. Of course, the authors of the Amendment could hardly have included telephone messages a hundred years before the device was invented. So it seemed obvious to Justice Brandeis that interpretations of the Constitution had to be made with awareness that "time works changes, brings into existence new conditions and purposes."

He added,

Subtler and more far-reaching means of invading privacy have become available to the government. Discovery and invention have made it possible for the government by means far more effective than stretching [a person] on the rack, to obtain disclosure in court of what is whispered in the closet.

Moreover, in the application of a Constitution, our contemplation cannot be only of what has been, but of what may be. The progress of science in furnishing the government with means of espionage is not likely to stop with wiretapping. Ways may some day be developed by which the government, without removing papers from secret drawers, can reproduce them in court, and by which it will be enabled to expose to a jury the most intimate occurrences of the home. Advances in the psychic and related sciences may bring means of exploring unexpressed beliefs, thoughts and emotions. "That places the liberty of every man in the hands of every petty officer" was said by James Otis of much lesser intrusions than these. . . .

Justice Brandeis felt that, indeed, tapping a telephone was "a far greater" invasion of privacy than opening mail. A wiretap, he observed, invades the privacy of two people in any given conversation. And over a period of time the tap of one man's phone invades the privacy of everyone he called and everyone who called him.

The dissenter strongly felt the Supreme Court's decision was wrong and that the lower court's verdict against Olmstead and his colleagues should be reversed. But more than that, Justice Brandeis deplored the idea set forth by Chief Justice Taft that ethics need play no part in how law officers obtained their evidence. This notion, Justice Brandeis felt, was insidious and if carried far enough could destroy the government itself. In concluding his dissenting opinion he not only offered eloquent support for the exclusionary rule, but provided future generations with words that would ring more and more true:

Decency, security, and liberty alike demand that government officials shall be subjected to the same rules of conduct that are commands to the citizen. In a government of laws, existence of the government will be imperiled if it fails to observe the law scrupulously. Our government is the potent, omnipresent teacher. For good or for ill, it teaches the whole people by its example. Crime is contagious. If the government becomes a law-breaker, it breeds contempt for law; it invites every man to become a law unto himself; it invites anarchy. To declare that in the administration of the criminal law the end justifies the means—to declare that the government may commit crimes in order to secure the conviction of a private criminal—would bring terrible retribution. Against that pernicious doctrine this Court should resolutely set its face.

These words of dissent, which would far outlive those uttered by Chief Justice Taft, were delivered June 4, 1928. It would be many years before the High Court adopted the concept implicit in Justice Brandeis's dissent, that all government officials, state as well as federal, should be commanded to abide by the Fourth Amendment.

5

Why the Police Cried Wolf

In the 1950s, if a state or city policeman like Sergeant Delau of Cleveland were told he couldn't search a home without a warrant, he might have "cried wolf"—to borrow a term used in this context by a lawyer familiar with the law of search and seizure. Knowingly or not, the officer would have been invoking the name of Dr. Julius A. Wolf, of Denver, Colorado. A Supreme Court case with his name guided state and local practices in search and seizure from 1949 until 1961.

It all began on April 25, 1944, when the district attorney's office in Denver received an anonymous telephone call revealing that in room 602 of the Cosmopolitan Hotel a woman was in serious trouble following an illegal abortion. Ray Humphries, the office's chief investigator, and his assistant, Louis Malach, hurried to the hotel, went up to room 602, and found Gertrude Martin, who was very ill. The officers, before taking her to the Denver General Hospital, learned that her pregnancy had, indeed, been aborted

by a Dr. A. H. Montgomery. She also revealed she had
been to see Dr. Wolf before and after the abortion.
Under state law, to perform or assist in performing an
abortion, except for certain medical reasons, was a
felony, a serious crime.

Two days later the district attorney's office decided
that on the basis of what had been learned from
Gertrude Martin, Dr. Wolf should be arrested.
Malach, who was also a deputy sheriff, and two deputy
district attorneys went to the doctor's office to pick him
up. They did not carry warrants, either for his arrest or
to search his office; nevertheless they found the
physician at his desk and arrested him. As they were
leading him from the office, one of the two investigators
noticed a couple of record books on a table. He picked
them up and took them along. They were "day books"
which contained the names of Dr. Wolf's patients and
what they had paid him.

As these records were studied back at the district
attorney's office, the investigators noted that certain
female patients had paid fees far, far greater than the
average. The officers guessed that these were pay-
ments for illegal abortions, so they contacted some of
the patients to ask about their exorbitant bills. The
interviews were extremely damaging to Drs. Wolf and
Montgomery and to another Denver doctor and his
wife.

Dr. Wolf was indicted under the state law, tried,
found guilty, and sentenced to the Colorado State
Penitentiary for "not less than 15 months or more than
5 years." He appealed to the State Supreme Court of
Colorado, where he lost. He then asked the Supreme
Court of the United States to hear his case, which the

High Court agreed to do. Technically, Dr. Wolf petitioned the Supreme Court to issue a "writ of certiorari" directing the Supreme Court of Colorado to send up the case's record for review by the Supreme Court of the United States. Under a federal law enacted in 1925, the High Court was given the right to grant or deny petitions for writs of certiorari. By granting Dr. Wolf's petition, the justices of the Supreme Court signaled that they wanted to review an issue concerning the Fourth Amendment raised by the case of *Wolf v. Colorado.*

In their legal application to the High Court for certiorari, Dr. Wolf's attorneys had presented the justices with a question that the Court had ducked in 1904 in the case of *Adams v. New York.* Forty-four years after the *Adams* decision, the High Court finally decided to confront the question.

As may be recalled, Albert Adams' attorneys had claimed that the Fourteenth Amendment to the Constitution commanded the High Court to make certain that no state deprive any citizen of his rights under the Bill of Rights. But deciding the case, the Court simply dodged the question, stating it did not "feel called upon to discuss" it.

While the main purpose of the Fourteenth Amendment, adopted in 1868, was to give the former slaves their citizenship, it was eventually interpreted far more widely. The reason for this was found in the next to the last clause of the Amendment's Section 1, the "due process" clause, which reads, ". . . nor shall any State deprive any person of life, liberty, or property, without due process of law. . . ." Arguably, these words may mean that such a liberty as the right to privacy could not be denied a person by the actions of a state, unless there were the fair and proper legal proceedings that are summed up in the words "due process."

As did the attorneys for Albert Adams, those for Dr. Wolf again raised the question in regard to what they labeled an illegal search and seizure by officers of the state of Colorado. They had come to the doctor's office with no warrant and seized the evidence that was sending him to jail. This, Dr. Wolf's lawyers argued, was first a violation of the Constitution of Colorado which plainly stated, "The People shall be secure in their persons, papers, homes and effects, from un-reasonable searches and seizures. . . ." Second, it violated the Fourth Amendment of the Constitution of the United States. The attorneys concluded that this clearly made the evidence illegal, and it should have been excluded from Dr. Wolf's trials. The due process clause of the Fourteenth Amendment, they argued, made it mandatory for the Supreme Court of the United States to keep the Colorado courts from depriving the physician of his right to privacy under the Fourth Amendment. The justices could reverse the state's decisions by forcing its courts to apply the exclusionary rule which had been used in federal courts for many years now.

The Supreme Court handed down its decision on June 27, 1949. Dr. Wolf won the argument about the Fourteenth Amendment, but the High Court refused to force the exclusionary rule upon the state, and the physician went to jail.

The decision, which came from a divided Court, was supported by majority opinion written by Justice Felix Frankfurter, who was appointed to the Supreme Court in 1939 by President Franklin D. Roosevelt. Justice Frankfurter was a physically small but peppery figure remembered for his pince-nez and the professorial look they gave him. Actually, he was a professor. Justice Frankfurter came from Harvard University, where he had taught law for twenty-five years. At that time he was known as a staunch follower of the liberal tradition, but on the Court he turned into one of the most conservative justices of the century. He was caught up by a philosophy of "judicial restraint" which maintained that the High Court should not unduly intrude upon the states or upon the other branches of the federal government. This philosophy was evident in the *Wolf* decision.

After an involved, sophisticated discussion of the "due process" clause of the Fourteenth Amendment, of where it could and where it shouldn't apply, Justice Frankfurter conceded that it should protect one's basic right of privacy against a state acting to deny it. He said:

The security of one's privacy against arbitrary intrusion by the police—which is at the core of the Fourth Amendment—is basic to a free society. It is therefore implicit in 'the concept of ordered liberty' and as such enforceable against the States through the Due Process Clause. The knock at the door, whether by day or by night, as a prelude to a search, without authority of law but solely on the authority of the police, did not need the commentary of recent history to be condemned as inconsistent with the conception of human rights enshrined in the history and the basic constitutional documents of English-speaking peoples.

63

If Dr. Wolf and his attorneys heard these words being read that June day of 1949, they must have thought they had won their case. The Court had finally decided that the Fourteenth Amendment did make it a constitutional violation for a state not to abide by the Fourth Amendment. To think that it wouldn't seemed to smack of the police state which Americans had just fought and died to prevent in the first half of the 1940s.

But then appellant Wolf and his lawyers, if they continued to listen, must have abruptly lost heart, because Justice Frankfurter's eloquent words were quickly followed by a large "but," after which he turned to his characteristic philosophy of being gentle in commanding the states what to do.

He built a case against the exclusionary rule in general and specifically as it pertained to whether the High Court should force it upon the states. The justice pointed out that the views of the states of the United States were not consistent with one another on the use of the exclusionary rule, which had been adopted in federal courts after the High Court's decision in *Weeks v. United States* of 1914. In support he offered a poll of how the question had been settled in the forty-six of the then forty-eight states whose courts had passed on the rule. Only sixteen had agreed with it, while thirty-one had rejected the idea.

Justice Frankfurter was also able to report on how the rule had been rejected in all ten jurisdictions of the United Kingdom and the British Commonwealth of Nations where the question had been passed upon. In every case the English courts were willing to accept evidence obtained by illegal searches and seizures.

The justice granted that the exclusionary rule was a

pretty effective means of preventing unreasonable searches—i.e., if evidence illegally seized weren't accepted it wouldn't be worth searching for—but he added that there were two sides to the argument over use of the rule. In the main the rule was "a remedy which directly serves only to protect those upon whose person or premises something incriminating has been found." In such instances the rule did not protect society because it prevented the illegally seized evidence from being used to convict criminals in court.

But how did Justice Frankfurter propose that state law officials be kept from practicing unreasonable searches and seizures in violation of the Fourth Amendment? Could a police-violator be sued for damages? Not very likely. Could the victim of an illegal search and seizure expect the officer conducting it to be demoted? Not very likely. The justice really didn't offer a creditable answer. In fact, his main reason was the most questionable of all. It was that in state and local cases of oppressive conduct by police, he felt that public opinion, "sporadically aroused," would be far more effective than any remote authority imposed by the federal government.

Wolf lost his case because the High Court refused to make Colorado courts exclude the illegally seized day books. The exclusionary rule was still applicable only to the federal government and not to the states, according to the decision. For most policemen in most states, it meant they really didn't have to bother with warrants and, if told otherwise, they could "cry Wolf."

Three justices voted against the *Wolf* decision, and their views were expressed in a vigorous dissenting opinion written by Justice Frank Murphy. He wrote:

65

It is disheartening to find so much that is right in an opinion [Frankfurter's] which seems to me so fundamentally wrong. . . . It is difficult for me to understand how the Court can go this far [in making the Fourth Amendment applicable to the states] and yet be unwilling to make the step [apply the exclusionary rule to the states] which can give some meaning to the pronouncement it utters.

Short of doing nothing, there were only three possible remedies to police violations of the Fourth Amendment, Justice Murphy explained:

• Excluding illegally obtained evidence from courts.
• Bringing criminal prosecution against officials violating the Amendment.
• Suing them for damages as trespassers.

The first, excluding the illegal evidence, was the only answer, Justice Murphy claimed. The other two were worthless alternatives.

To expect a policeman to police himself or a prosecutor to prosecute himself for criminal violations of the Fourth Amendment was ridiculed by the dissenter. "Self-scrutiny is a lofty ideal," he said, "but its [praise] reaches new heights if we expect a District Attorney to prosecute himself or his associates for well-meaning violations of the search and seizure clause during a raid the District Attorney or his Associates have ordered."

The justice then pointed out that in a trespass action in court the trespasser can only be sued for injury to physical property. This was also ridiculed by saying, "If the officer searches with care, he can avoid all but nominal damages—a penny, or a dollar."

After exploring other even less practical ways of punishing officials for illegally searching and seizing evidence, Justice Murphy stated:

> The Conclusion is inescapable that but one remedy exists to deter violations of the search and seizure clause [the Fourth Amendment]. That is the rule which excludes illegally obtained evidence. Only by exclusion can we impress upon the zealous prosecutor that violation of the Constitution will do him no good. And only when that point is driven home can the prosecutor be expected to emphasize the importance of observing constitutional demands in his instructions to the police.

While these words may have had an argument-winning ring to them, they did not win the case for Dr. Wolf. The rule of the Court's majority remained, as it had since the Adams case of 1904, against forcing the exclusionary rule upon state courts.

With one very strange exception this decision was to continue as the law of the land for another thirteen years. The exception was a case brought to the Supreme Court by Antonio Richard Rochin.

On July 1, 1949, three deputy sheriffs of the county of Los Angeles suspected that Rochin was selling narcotics, and they went to his house to investigate. The door was open, so the sheriffs walked in and went upstairs to a bedroom where Rochin had locked himself in with his wife. He wouldn't open the door, so the lawmen forced it open and confronted the suspect, who was seated on the bed.

Immediately the deputies noticed two capsules on a nightstand beside Rochin, and one of the officers asked, "Whose stuff is that?"

Rochin didn't reply, but grabbed the capsules and put them in his mouth. The sheriffs jumped on him and tried to extract the capsules, but Rochin swallowed them. The suspect was then subdued, handcuffed, and hauled off to a hospital where, under a sheriff's orders, a doctor pumped the suspect's stomach against his will. It caused vomiting and the two capsules were thrown up. They contained morphine, and on this evidence Rochin was found guilty of violating a California narcotics law.

The Californian appealed his conviction all the way to the Supreme Court of the United States. In January 1952, the High Court handed down its decision with an opinion written by Justice Frankfurter.

This time, despite the justice's firm philosophy of not imposing the rule of exclusion on a state court, the facts of the bizarre search and seizure were too much to accept and he wrote:

> . . . we are compelled to conclude that the proceedings by which this conviction was obtained do more than offend some fastidious squeamishness or private sentimentalism about combatting crime too energetically. This is conduct that shocks the conscience. Illegally breaking into the privacy of the petitioner [Rochin], the struggle to open his mouth and remove what was there, the

forcible extraction of his stomach contents—this course of proceeding by agents of government to obtain evidence is found to offend even hardened sensibilities. They are methods too close to the rack and the screw to permit. . . .

The actions of the state courts against Rochin were reversed, and he went free. Essentially, it was a case of the Supreme Court imposing the exclusionary rule on a state court, but Justice Frankfurter made it clear that this decision was to be viewed as an exception and not as a precedent. The states, he intimated, could continue employing illegal evidence obtained "through the use of modern methods and devices for discovering wrongdoers and bringing them to book." Such methods were not to be compared with those used against Rochin, "so brutal and so offensive to human dignity in securing evidence."

Justice William O. Douglas concurred in the *Rochin* decision, but he spoke disdainfully of the reasoning behind the decision. First of all, he couldn't understand what seemed to him like a double standard for use of the exclusionary rule. "If it is a requirement of due process in the federal courthouse," he said, "it is impossible for me to say it is not a requirement of due process for a trial in the state courthouse."

Then he continued that *all* evidence illegally obtained from a person should be excluded from state trials. To force the states to exclude some evidence because certain Supreme Court justices felt it was against the "decencies of civilized conduct" and yet allow them to use other illegal evidence was wrong, Justice Douglas maintained. "That is to make the [exclusionary] rule turn not on the Constitution but on the idiosyncrasies of the judges who sit here," he declared.

He said he saw this kind of thinking in other recent cases and he feared, "It is part of the process of erosion of civil rights of the citizen in recent years."

But for another nine years the *Rochin* decision remained an exception to the Court's position against making state courts exclude evidence obtained in violation of the Fourth Amendment. However, in those years the composition and philosophy of the High Court changed considerably. A year after *Rochin*, President Dwight D. Eisenhower appointed Earl Warren as chief justice, and the great tribunal of last resorts soon evolved into the famous Warren Court. As much as ever in the history of the Supreme Court, the justices sitting with Earl Warren, a former politician who had been governor of California, became concerned with protecting the rights of citizens through the Bill of Rights.

This concern was eventually to reach out to Dollree Mapp of Cleveland—and to everyone else who might become the victim of searches and seizures that violated the Fourth Amendment.

6

Against Ohio's Peace and Dignity

Dollree Mapp was destined to spend many nights and days in prison. Her first imprisonment, for only a single night, occurred on Thursday, May 23, 1957, the day her home was searched by the Cleveland police without their showing her a warrant. When the search was over, Sergeant Carl Delau of the Special Investigations Bureau and his assistants, Michael Haney and Thomas Dever, had two sets of evidence with which to bring charges against Ms. Mapp. They had a number of lottery tickets and other "paraphernalia" used in the illegal game of "policy," and they had books and pictures which they knew would be considered obscene literature.

The possession of lottery tickets was a misdemeanor, a relatively minor offense, which would bring only a small fine. But the mere possession of obscene literature was an entirely different story. In Ohio, at the time, this act was a felony, a very serious crime, which could result in a fine up to $2,000 or a jail sentence of one to seven years.

With Dollree Mapp under arrest and riding in the

back of their patrol car, Sergeant Delau and his colleagues drove from her neighborhood to downtown Cleveland and the city's police station. There, around 5:30 or 6:00 that evening, she was booked by the police, given a meal, and placed in a cell for the night.

From the next morning, Friday, May 24, until Monday the 27, Ms. Mapp was caught up in legal activity at the lowest level of America's judicial systems. She went before a municipal court—or police court—which had authority to deal only with the least serious of cases, such as traffic violations.

Here, on Friday, she was finally represented by her attorney, Al Kearns. He had been in another court the previous afternoon when his partner's son, the young attorney Walter Greene, had tried unsuccessfully to help her. Kearns, in his late fifties or early sixties, was an athletically built, square-shouldered man who loved to hunt and fish in the country, though most of the time his practice held him in the sprawling city of Cleveland. To those who worked with him, he was a kind man and soft-spoken. But others saw him as a crusty, old-time lawyer fully capable of dealing with the tough, hard realities of criminal law in Cleveland. The attorney was usually dressed in a conservative business suit, coarsely woven but well-tailored, and he often wore a single flower in his left lapel.

He was certainly comfortable at the Cleveland Municipal Court on the second floor of the city's police station. Many of his cases began, and frequently ended, right there before a judge, who was also called a magistrate. The principals of the court and the police department knew and respected Kearns as one of the city's busy criminal lawyers.

In his visit to the police station that Friday morning the attorney learned from Dollree Mapp and the police as much as he could about what had happened the previous day. He added this to what he had already found out from Walter Greene, and then prepared to get his client released from jail and, if possible, free of the charges against her as quickly as he could.

That day she was charged with the misdemeanor of possession of "policy paraphernalia." At the same time Cleveland newspapers were reporting that the Thursday afternoon "raid" led by Sergeant Delau on the Mapp house had produced such paraphernalia, and it was said to be related to the bombing investigation which had led Delau to Ms. Mapp. The press quoted the officer as saying the raid had turned up a "trunk" containing policy slips, records, and other equipment once used in a gambling house known as California Gold, which had been shut down a month earlier.

With little trouble Kearns convinced a magistrate that the policy material had nothing to do with the bombing, nor did it belong to Dollree Mapp. The case was dismissed and she was discharged. Around the same time Virgil Ogletree, who had been arrested at her house, was released free of any charges.

Over the weekend, however, a new and more serious charge was filed against Ms. Mapp. It was spelled out in an affidavit (a written statement sworn to under oath) prepared by officer Michael Haney. It charged her with the "Possession of Obscene Pictures & Books." With this paper the policeman obtained a court warrant for Ms. Mapp's arrest, and on Monday she was rearrested and brought back to the Municipal Court to be arraigned (accused and given a chance to answer her accusers) before Judge Andrew Kovachy.

Kearns, who was at the arraignment, could have asked for, and probably received, a hearing for his client, but as he considered the charge and the evidence being used to back it up, the attorney concluded he would be wasting everyone's time. He recognized that the books and pictures seized by the police on Thursday offered "prima facie evidence" (established on first appearances) that the charge was valid. Regardless of what he or Ms. Mapp might say about it, the evidence gave Judge Kovachy "probable cause" to order that the case be pursued. Kearns said nothing and advised Ms. Mapp to do the same.

Judge Kovachy knew, however, that the crime charged was beyond his court's "jurisdiction" (legal authority). The crime being a felony, it would have to be taken up in the next higher state court, the Court of Common Pleas of Cuyahoga County (the county in which Cleveland is located). Judge Kovachy also knew that in moving upward, the accusation would have to be weighed en route by the county's grand jury. Therefore—to use legal jargon—he "bound over" the case to the grand jury's next session. In the meantime Ms. Mapp could go free only by putting up bail (money deposited at the court with the understanding it would be forfeited should she fail to appear when called). At Kearns' request, the judge set the bail at $2,500, and when the proper financial arrangements were made, the accused woman was released. She went home and waited to see what would happen when her case came before the next grand jury.

Historically grand juries were established so that citizen jurors (of "twelve to twenty-three good and lawful persons") could carefully weigh and approve or reject the accusations of government officials. Grand juries have always met secretly so they could assess information that might be false and unfairly damaging to the accused if it were discussed publicly. If the jurors, by a majority vote, decided that the government had sufficient reason to charge a person with a crime, they could then "indict" (formally accuse) the person. Then the case would probably go to trial before a judge and a "petit" (little) jury, usually of twelve jurors, who would hear the government's evidence to support the indictment and the person's defense (which is why the person is often called the "defendant"). The twelve jurors would then decide on the defendant's guilt or innocence.

In Cleveland the official who would now represent the government (the state) before the grand jury was the prosecuting attorney of Cuyahoga County, John T. Corrigan. The Municipal Court sent the Mapp case to him, and he waited to take it to the grand jury, which would be impaneled (its newest membership enrolled) in September.

When the time came, Corrigan appeared in the secret session before the grand jurors, who numbered fifteen. He read them the charge and told them about the evidence that the police had found in Dollree Mapp's home back in May. That was all that the jurors heard. The onesidedness of the action was excusable because of the nature of a grand jury. It was convened not to decide guilt or innocence, but only to determine whether there was sufficient evidence to bring her case to trial. From what the jurors could gather on the face of the situation there was probable cause to accuse

75

Dollree Mapp formally—and they did so by voting in favor of issuing an "Indictment for Possession of Obscene Literature." When printed, it read as follows:

Of the term of September In the year of our Lord one thousand nine hundred and fifty seven.

The Jurors of the Grand Jury of the State of Ohio, within and for the body of the County aforesaid, on their oaths, IN THE NAME AND BY THE AUTHORITY OF THE STATE OF OHIO,

Do Find and Present, That Dolly Mapp on or about the 23rd day of May 1957, at the County aforesaid, unlawfully and knowingly had in her possession and under her control, certain lewd and lascivious Books, Pictures and Photographs, said Books, Pictures and Photographs being so indecent and immoral in their nature that the same would be offensive to the Court and improper to be placed upon the records thereof contrary to the form of the statute in such case made and provided, and against the peace and dignity of the State of Ohio.

Shortly after this indictment was filed with the Court of Common Pleas by Prosecuting Attorney Corrigan, Dollree Mapp was called upon to plead guilty or not guilty before a judge. On Kearns' advice she pleaded not guilty. The accused then began one of the longest of several long waiting periods in the course of the case, which was now titled: *The State of Ohio v. Dollree Mapp*, Case No. 68326. Nearly a year went by before it was actually brought to trial before a petit jury of twelve citizens.

During that year Dollree Mapp continued living with her daughter at Milverton Road. She attended adult education classes in a nearby public school, attempting to complete the high school education she had never finished. She was also learning interior decorating while working part time in a decorating shop.

But during these months Ms. Mapp couldn't forget that she faced a terribly serious indictment for a felony which could bring a drastic penalty. She also realized that to fight her case could be tremendously expensive. Lawyers like Kearns and his firm commanded hourly fees that could add up to staggering sums of money, considering all the time that it required such professionals to prepare for and appear in one's behalf in court. It was a crushing burden for the young woman, and it was made worse by her feelings that the charges were completely unfair. She felt she had been framed with evidence, illegally obtained, which should never have been used against her, no matter how it was found and taken by the police.

Also, Dollree Mapp couldn't help but assume that she was a victim of racial discrimination. Had she been a white woman, she believed, her legal circumstances might have been different. Because she was black, she felt the police had gone out of their way to get something on her. They had come to her home looking for someone connected with a bombing, but had left with evidence on an entirely separate, extraneous matter—all without producing a warrant specifying what they were searching for. The accused woman realized that her refusal to let the officers into her house certainly could have made them angry with her, but her color, she was convinced, had turned their ire into a vicious attempt to put her in jail.

In these troubled months Ms. Mapp claims she had a friend who believed both in her and in her assumption that the police action had been racially motivated. He was a white businessman, an older person, who was relatively wealthy. She claims that this person, who remained anonymous, was deeply sensitive to the suffering of black people in America. When he learned of Ms. Mapp's legal problems, he sympathized with her plight and began paying her legal expenses.

"He would never pay the bills directly," she explains, "but when a lawyer's bill came I would send it to him, he would give me the amount that was due, and I would pay it. Without his help I never would have been able to fight the case at all."

As the year went by, Dollree Mapp frequently called Al Kearns to find out when she could expect her case to go to trial. It could be many months, the lawyer explained, for the court's docket was crowded with dozens of cases of which No. 68326 was well down the list. In the meantime, Kearns assured her he was preparing her defense and he felt she, as the defendant, had a pretty good chance of winning, in light of the facts surrounding what had happened on May 23.

By July 1958, Kearns expected the case to go to trial in September, and on the last day of July the lawyer initiated the first of many legal moves that he would make to bring the proceedings against Dollree Mapp to a close in her favor. Most of these moves were technical

78

actions designed to persuade a court—in the person of one or more judges—to decide the case for the accused woman, thus terminating the costly, worrisome legal proceedings that would occur should the case run its full course. Convincing a judge that he could legally do so and that the lawyer's proposed move would best serve the cause of justice was, of course, the key to success. Such legal capability is what clients need and what they often pay for handsomely.

On July 31 Kearns appeared in the Common Pleas Court and made a proposal before the bench of Judge Joseph A. Artl. The lawyer said that if the judge would promise to levy no more than a fine against Ms. Mapp, he, as her attorney, would recommend that she change her plea of not guilty to guilty. He was trying what is known as "plea bargaining."

Kearns felt that with the extremely crowded court docket, the offer to settle the Mapp case quickly and easily with a simple decision by the judge might be attractive to everyone concerned. It could avoid a long, costly trial by jury. The state, in effect, would win its case. The accused would go free after paying a fine, which under the law couldn't exceed $2,000. The judge, Kearns argued, could legally make such a decision, and the cause of justice would be served all around.

Judge Artl asked for comment on the recommendation from a lawyer who had joined the conference at the bench, representing the prosecuting attorney's office. The lawyer didn't believe the state would favor such a decision, whereupon the judge rejected Kearns' recommendation.

Ohio v. Mapp was scheduled for trial September 3,

1958, in the Criminal Branch of the Court of Common Pleas. The title of the court, used widely in the United States, was a carry-over from the earliest English courts where cases brought by citizens were called "common pleas." In the case at hand the original meaning no longer held—as revealed in the title, *Ohio v. Mapp*, in which the government was bringing the plea.

7

In the Bedroom
or the Basement

The trial of Dollree Mapp went practically unnoticed in Cleveland because it was looked upon by the press as a "dirty little smut case," a minor criminal case among scores tried in the busy Cuyahoga County court in a year. It took place in one of a number of small, dark, oak-paneled courtrooms in the Criminal Branch of the Court of Common Pleas in downtown Cleveland.

A little before ten on Wednesday morning, September 3, 1958, the parties to the case appeared in the courtroom where, at the moment, there were only a couple of uniformed guards. The state's lawyer, assigned from the county prosecutor's office, was Gertrude Bauer Mahon, a middle-aged woman, with reddish hair and of medium height and build. She was the assistant prosecuting attorney of Cuyahoga County. Ms. Mahon would present the case of the plaintiff (the state of Ohio) against the defendant (Dollree Mapp) and then try to support it with evidence. Ms. Mahon arrived with a well-packed briefcase and sat at one of two tables in front of the judge's bench.

She was immediately followed into the room by

Sergeant Carl Delau and Patrolman Michael Haney. Both were in civilian clothes. They greeted Ms. Mahon and sat down behind her.

Shortly Dollree Mapp, accompanied by two women, arrived with attorney Kearns. One of the women was a friend who had come to observe the proceedings, but the other was a possible witness, Delores Clark. Kearns, as usual, was meticulously dressed in a light-gray suit with a vest and a fresh white flower in his lapel. In a few minutes he was joined by Walter Greene, who had only recently become a partner in the law firm established by his father and Kearns. But Greene wasn't present as an attorney. He came as a witness.

Kearns, also carrying a briefcase, greeted Ms. Mahon, and then sat at a table next to the one she had taken. Greene and the three women sat in chairs directly behind the tables. They were in the same row as Delau and Haney. All of them were in front of a small section of seats for the public—none of which were occupied.

Just before the proceedings were to start, two court officials arrived, greeted the attorneys, and took their places at the front of the raised bench. One was a man assigned to the case from the office of the clerk of the court. The other, a woman, was a court stenographer who would make a record of the trial. Shortly after ten o'clock a door at the side of the courtroom opened, the clerk commanded that everyone rise, and the judge assigned to the case entered. He wore the traditional black robe, and as he walked rapidly up to his chair behind the bench, the bottom of the robe opened briefly, revealing that underneath the black covering the man wore an ordinary business suit. That glimpse added a human touch to an otherwise austere, magisterial scene.

The judge, one of a number serving the Court of Common Pleas, had been assigned for the trial of Case No. 68326. He was the Honorable Donald F. Lybarger. He sat down and so did everyone else, and then there was a minute's silence as Judge Lybarger sifted through some papers that had been placed on his bench by the clerk.

"This is the matter of the state of Ohio versus Dollree Mapp," the judge suddenly announced, breaking the silence of the imposing room. He looked at Kearns and then at Ms. Mahon as he continued, "The defendant and counsel are in court; the prosecutor is in court."

The judge took up a paper from those before him.

"I have before me a motion to suppress evidence," he announced. Looking toward Kearns, he then asked, "Mr. Kearns, you bring that on behalf of the defendant?"

Al Kearns stood up. "Yes," he replied. "May it please your Honor, this motion to suppress the evidence in this case is based upon Section 2905.35 of the Ohio Revised Code [a state law], which became effective October 6, 1955; the statute under which the defendant has been indicted [2905.34, the state obscenity law] became effective October 6, 1955. . . ."

Having established that the two laws had been passed the same day, Kearns pointed out that 2905.35 specified that warrants could be issued to search "a building or other place" where "obscene items" might be located.

"Now we say," Kearns went on, "that the state of

Ohio did not have a search warrant setting forth the items that are mentioned in this indictment, and which the state of Ohio intends to use as evidence in this case against this defendant, and for that reason we are asking that that particular evidence be suppressed."

If Judge Lybarger had accepted Kearns' motion and if the judge's decision had been allowed to stand, unappealed by the state's attorney, the case would have been settled in favor of Ms. Mapp. The evidence, the obscene books and pictures, would not have been admitted to the trial, so the state would no longer have had a case. But it didn't happen that way. Judge Lybarger overruled the motion. He didn't say so, but probably he was relying on the ancient common-law rule of moving forward to seek the truth of a case without stopping to argue over the origins of the evidence.

With this business done, prospective jurors were brought into the room and twelve were selected to hear the case—six men and six women, as it turned out. The bulk of the trial was held on September 3 and it was completed the following day.

After short opening statements by Ms. Mahon and Kearns explaining what they intended to prove, witnesses were heard. Those called by Ms. Mahon for the state came first.

Patrolman Haney was the first to be put on the witness stand. Ms. Mahon's questions elicited his version of what happened at Dollree Mapp's house some fifteen months past. Essentially, the testimony was that the police had found obscene books and photographs in Ms. Mapp's bedroom.

The prosecuting attorney then brought forth the

items that had been seized, and she handled each as if it had just been lifted from a sewer.

"Officer," she said, presenting Haney with the first on the pile, "showing you what is identified as State's Exhibit 1, what can you tell me about that?"

"That," replied Haney, "is a book entitled *The Affairs of the Troubadour*. It has my initials, M. H.; the date '5-23-57.' It was one of the books found in the dresser drawer on this date."

Ms. Mahon produced three other small books, which she identified as State's Exhibits 2, 3, and 4, and with each she and Haney went through the same line of questions and answers. The books in the order presented had the suggestive titles that follow: *Little Darlings, London Stage Affairs,* and *Memories of a Hotel Man.* All of them, according to Haney, had been found in a dresser drawer in Ms. Mapp's bedroom.

Ms. Mahon then produced five more exhibits, numbered 5 through 9. The first was described by Haney as "a piece of paper with some obscene drawings on it in pencil." He claimed that this was found in a suitcase beside Ms. Mapp's bed. The remaining four exhibits included a doctor's diet slip made out to Ms. Mapp, a personal legal paper with her name on it, and two photographs of Dollree Mapp with two friends at a place called the Chatterbox Musical Bar and Grill. The patrolman said all of the items had been found with the dirty drawing in the suitcase.

Four more exhibits were produced, numbers 10 through 13, and the officer identified each as an "obscene photo." He claimed they had been found by Sergeant Delau in a chest of drawers in the Mapp home.

Next, lawyer Kearns cross-examined Haney and tried to destroy the impression left by the officer that all the obscene items were found in Ms. Mapp's apartment with other items (such as the diet slip) identifiable as hers. For instance, the lawyer grilled Haney about the suitcase and what came out of it.

"Now in the suitcase," he asked, "weren't there other things besides the photographs you spoke of? Wasn't there a man's shirt in that suitcase?"

"No, there was not," said Haney.

"Wasn't there anything pertaining to men's clothing in the suitcase?" asked Kearns somewhat incredulously.

"No, sir."

"Nothing?"

"Nothing."

"Did you talk to Mrs. Mapp about that particular suitcase, as to whom it belonged to?"

"Yes, we did."

"And she told you it belonged to her?"

"Yes, she did."

"What else, if anything, did she tell you?"

"Nothing."

"Didn't she tell you she had loaned the suitcase to Morris Jones, to put things in there?"

"No, she did not."

Morris Jones, according to Ms. Mapp, had been a tenant in her house. She had given up her bedroom for the income and had moved into her daughter's room. Jones had left the obscene materials when he had recently departed for New York, claimed the owner of the house.

Kearns continued trying to establish that Haney had

ignored other items in the suitcase, which had obviously belonged to Jones. The attorney asked if was true that a textbook of cosmetology (the cosmetic arts, skin care, hairdressing, etc.) had been in the bag, and that Jones's name had been written on it. Haney denied ever having seen the book.

Kearns then opened a line of questions about when Haney had truly found the diet slip. "And isn't it a fact that that diet slip was not found in the suitcase but in the drawer of the desk in the living room?" asked Kearns.

"No, it is not a fact," answered Haney. "It was found in the suitcase."

The defense lawyer then brought up a key question with respect to the obscene books. "Now, officer," he said, "I want you to tell this jury, isn't it a fact that some obscene matters were found in a box in the basement where the lottery slips were found?"

"Not to my knowledge," Haney responded. "Anything they found and presented here was found in the bedroom."

"Didn't you learn that some things were found in the box?"

"Nothing obscene; there was no box found other than the trunk, the policy paraphernalia."

"That was in the basement, wasn't it?"

"Yes."

"And in that box where the policy paraphernalia was found was a small brown bag with most of this evidence you have introduced here and state you found; isn't that true, to your knowledge?"

"Objection!" Ms. Mahon interrupted.

"He may answer," stated the judge, overruling her.

"That is not true," replied Haney.

Later Kearns questioned Haney about whether or not there had been a search warrant. The patrolman claimed that one had been obtained.

"Where is that search warrant?" asked Kearns.

"I don't know," said Haney.

"Do you have it here?"

"I don't have it here."

"Would you tell the jury who has it?"

"I can't tell the jury who has it; no, sir."

"And you were one of the investigating officers in the investigation by the police department?"

"Yes."

"But you can't tell us where the search warrant is?"

"No, I cannot."

"Or what it recites?"

"No."

Ms. Mahon then put Sergeant Delau on the stand and had him review the circumstances of the search. He supported Patrolman Haney in maintaining that the obscene materials had all been found in Dollree Mapp's bedroom. Delau claimed they had seen "no men's clothing at all in that particular bedroom." They did not find any of the obscene items in the basement, the sergeant claimed. He said that a search warrant had been obtained and brought to the Mapp house by a Lieutenant White. Kearns' cross-examination of the officer was relatively mild, and didn't add or detract from Haney's testimony.

Haney and Delau being the only witnesses for the state, it was time for Kearns to put his defense witnesses on the stand. The first was his young partner, Walter Greene, who told of what he saw at the Mapp house on the afternoon of the raid. Kearns, pointing to Sergeant Delau in the courtroom, asked if this was the officer the young attorney had seen breaking into their client's house.

"Yes," said Greene, ". . . I stopped and asked him what they were doing; he said they wanted to get in. I asked if they had a warrant; if they had a warrant it wasn't necessary [to break in]; just show it to Mrs. Mapp. He said he had a warrant; they refused to show it to anybody. I never did see a warrant."

"Go ahead," Kearns urged, "and tell it to the court, what happened."

"The sergeant tried, as I say, to kick in the door, and she wouldn't come down. Then he got a sharp instrument—I mean a metallic instrument; I don't know what it was—and broke the glass in the door and somebody reached in and opened the door and let them in."

Kearns, by his questioning of Greene, also made it clear that Ms. Mapp was denied the lawyer's counsel during the raid. Greene had not been allowed in the house. Kearns had already established this fact in his earlier cross-examination of the two policemen.

The defense attorney next called Delores Clark, the woman who had come to court as a witness for Ms. Mapp. She was a friend who had occasionally helped Ms. Mapp keep house. She told of working there one day soon after Morris Jones had left. Some of his belongings, she explained, were packed in a box and stored in the basement. Asked what went into the box, Ms. Clark responded in a feeble voice. "Men's clothes. A lot of junk, letters, shoes, just general stuff, [we] put them in. . . ."

"You have to speak a little louder," said Kearns.

"When we got the stuff up off the floor," said the witness, "and put it in the box, we started to clean out the dresser drawer, and all of a sudden she [Ms. Mapp] had this bag, a brown paper bag; she opened it up, she said, 'Look what's in here.' Then when she took the stuff out of the bag it was a bunch of dirty books and some pictures. She said, 'Look at what filthy stuff men read.' So we laughed it off, put it in the bag, and put it with the man's stuff."

"You put it in the bag with the man's stuff?"

"Yes."

"And where, if you remember, did you take the bag eventually?"

"We took the whole bunch of junk down in the basement."

Kearns showed the woman the four books, Exhibits 1 through 4, and she agreed they could have been in the bag that went to the basement. She also felt the obscene photographs had been in the bag.

Finally Kearns put Dollree Mapp on the stand. Answering question after question, she told the often-repeated story of the break-in, of how she held off the raiders, of how she had snatched a paper, supposedly a warrant, away from the police but that they had wrestled it away from her, and of how she had been handcuffed while the officers searched her home.

She claimed that while Sergeant Delau was going through her bedroom, Patrolman Haney suddenly walked in with a brown bag.

"Walked in from where?" asked Kearns.

"I don't know where he came from," said Ms. Mapp, "but he walked into my bedroom door, and he said,

'Does this belong to you?' I asked him not to look at it, it might embarrass him. He asked me again if it belonged to me. I said, 'No.' He said, 'Oh, yes, that's the kind of trash you read.' "

The defendant was then led to explain that the contents of the bag had belonged to Morris Jones, that she and Delores Clark had put the bag in a box and stored it in the basement. Through extensive questioning that followed, Kearns built up support for the contention that the officers found none of the damaging evidence with Dollree Mapp's belongings, but, in truth, had discovered them with personal belongings left by the roomer, Jones. The attorney also elicited an oral portrait of the police making a wide-ranging search of the Mapp house, even to the point of taking some of the defendant's daughter's crayons.

"Were you ever given an opportunity to read the search warrant?" asked Kearns.

"I never had—I never read one word on there," replied the accused woman.

Ms. Mahon vigorously cross-examined Dollree Mapp, asking her a total of one hundred and ten questions. Most were designed to show that much of Ms. Mapp's testimony was contrary to that from the police. At one point, in response to a question, Ms. Mapp accused the police of lying. The reply made clear that someone was lying, but the prosecuting attorney wanted the jury to decide it was Ms. Mapp.

When the cross-examination was done, Kearns announced "that the defense rests," and the testimony and presentation of evidence was over. Then followed some legal maneuvers that included a motion by Kearns. The lawyer called upon Judge Lybarger to decide then and there that the state had failed to make its case—in which event the judge would "direct" a verdict of "not guilty." The motion was promptly overruled. Finally, after brief statements to the jury by both attorneys, the judge gave the jurors the "Charge of the Court." In the long and complicated statement he instructed the jurors on the law that governed the case.

"It . . . becomes your duty," he said, "to accept the law as this court gives it to you, to adopt it as a guide for your determination of what the facts actually are in this matter, and by that means to arrive at a verdict which will be just and fair."

He then offered the jurors a number of lessons: on the nature of evidence, the meaning of the indictment, the presumption of the defendant's innocence until the jurors had removed from their minds every reasonable doubt to the contrary, the burden of the state of proving her guilty, and the need to acquit Ms. Mapp if a reasonable doubt remained as to her guilt. These lessons were standard for judges instructing juries in such cases, and Judge Lybarger knew them virtually by heart. The second half of the charge, however, became specific as to the law that was allegedly violated. The judge read the particular section that the accused was said to have broken and then he virtually defined the words and phrases so there would be no misunderstanding of what the legal terminology was all about.

"One final word, ladies and gentlemen," the judge added in conclusion. "This case is of great importance to the state, and it is of great importance to the defendant, Dollree Mapp. You as citizens and jurors are now called on to decide the important question of the guilt or innocence of the accused. It is essential for the welfare of society that those who are guilty of crime should be found guilty, but it is also essential that anyone that is innocent should be found innocent. So I charge you to deliberate carefully, in accordance with your oath, and to return a verdict which will respond to the facts in the case as you find them to be, and the law as this court has given it to you.

"Is there anything further?" the judge asked for the last time, looking at the two attorneys.

"No, your Honor," said Ms. Mahon.

"Nothing on behalf of the defense, your Honor," Kearns replied.

The jury was out only forty-five minutes, and it returned a verdict of guilty. Shortly thereafter Dollree Mapp, who was practically knocked senseless by what she heard, was given the maximum sentence under the Ohio law: seven years in the Ohio Reformatory for Women at Marysville.

8

She Loses: Four for Her and Three Against

After Dollree Mapp was sentenced, Al Kearns announced her intention to appeal, and Judge Lybarger allowed her to remain free on bail in the meantime. Now freedom took on a new and deeper meaning because it had a possible bad ending not too far away. The future held the clear, ever-present threat of seven years in jail. Ms. Mapp avoided thinking of what it would be like, and as the shock of the sentencing wore off, she assumed more and more that she would successfully avoid serving time at Marysville.

Fortunately, the sizable sums of money for legal fees to keep her free continued to be available. The wealthy businessman, the anonymous donor of lawyers' costs, agreed to continue his support so she could appeal her conviction. As these months passed, Ms. Mapp learned firsthand that justice is more likely to come to those who can afford it than to those who can't—and the price can be extremely high because it buys sophisticated, expensive legal skills.

From the time he started handling the case, including before, during, and at the very end of the trial, Kearns had carefully developed the basis for an appeal in the event they lost in the Court of Common Pleas. With the verdict of guilty only hours old, he made one last effort to reverse the decision, and this, too, became a possible foundation stone for the forthcoming appeal. Here's what he did:

On September 6 Kearns returned to Judge Lybarger's bench and filed a motion for a new trial. He offered eight reasons why the trial completed only forty-eight hours earlier had failed to do justice for his client.

He argued that the jury's verdict and the judge's judgment were contrary both to the evidence and to the law. Furthermore, he maintained that the obscenity law itself was unconstitutional, and that Ms. Mapp's "constitutional right to due process of law" had been denied her.

Then Kearns accused the court (the judge) of making a series of errors that he claimed interfered with justice. The attorney claimed the court erred in not rejecting the evidence, the obscene items, even before the trial started. The court erred again, he claimed, by admitting the evidence over his objection when the trial was under way. These and other errors, he said, were reason enough for Judge Lybarger to give Dollree Mapp a new trial.

As Kearns expected, the judge quickly overruled the motion. Still, the attorney had again exercised one of the important functions of his profession—laying the foundations for a successful appeal. The "errors" that a judge may make in the difficult and delicate matter of conducting a fair and impartial trial can often serve as the basis of an appeal. Higher courts do not retry the original case with new testimony and evidence. They

96

review the conduct of the trial and the judgment of the lower courts to see if the loser was, indeed, fairly tried under the law. Thus appeals judges focus on the lower courts' possible errors. A good attorney does two things to pave the way for an appeal:

• He makes certain, through his motions, which are often numerous and made at every turn of the proceedings, that the judge is urged to do everything he should to ensure a fair trial. When the judge denies a reasonably sound motion, it becomes a potential error for review by higher courts.

• The lawyer sees to it that the possible errors are clearly spelled out in the record of the case—as Kearns did when he called for a new trial.

With the overruling of his last motion, everything was now done that he could do in the Court of Common Pleas, so Kearns turned to the next higher state court, the Eighth District Court of Appeals in Ohio. On September 26 he filed a "Notice of Appeal" for Ms. Mapp and, as in his motion for a new trial, the notice included a list of errors "complained of" by Dollree Mapp. They were essentially the same as in the last motion to Judge Lybarger, except one had been added, saying, "That the Court erred and deprived defendant of her constitutional guarantees in that cruel and unusual punishment was inflicted." Here Kearns was preparing to argue that the seven-year sentence for such an offense should be considered "cruel and unusual punishment," therefore violating the constitutions of both Ohio and the United States.

In mid-November 1958 the Cleveland attorney filed an extensive brief (legal statement) with the appeals court, a small panel of judges in Cleveland. There he described and discussed the Mapp case in general and then he went into specific arguments in support of the errors he had said were made in the lower court. Here, in the appeal, the title of the case was reversed, becoming *Mapp v. Ohio* because Dollree Mapp was now taking the action against the state.

If one were guided only by the severe judgment of that court, said Kearns, he might expect to find that the record of the trial would show that Ms. Mapp had a store selling pornographic merchandise for profit, complete with window displays to lure the customers. On the contrary, he continued, the police broke into a private home without a warrant; they weren't after obscene materials, and finding any at all was only incidental to the search. He continued: "There were from seven to twelve police officers involved; they came . . . to find some man for questioning as to a bombing, which some unknown said might be at the address. No such man was there. . . ."

Kearns went on to argue that, in any event, "there was no possession or control by Dollree Mapp" of the obscene articles seized by the police. The record of the case, said Kearns, had no indications of a vicious act on his client's part—such as being a seller or exhibitor of obscene literature, "who caters to depraved minds. The books and pictures were not her property," he maintained, "but of a roomer—they were packed away to await his disposition."

Kearns cited several court decisions involving people who had been accused of possessing illegal liquor left on their properties by employees or tenants in circumstances like those in the Mapp case, yet the courts had decided no "possession or control" existed.

The same should have applied to Dollree Mapp, her lawyer concluded.

Next he attacked the instructions that Judge Lybarger had given the jury at the end of the trial. Kearns complained that the trial judge had implied in a key sentence that in storing the roomer's property Ms. Mapp had, in fact, hidden the obscene articles.

"One who deposits articles in a place of concealment," the judge had said, "may still be deemed to have them in his possession."

This and other misuses of words, argued Kearns, confused and misled the jury into thinking that his client was legally the possessor of the articles "for a guilty purpose." In other similar cases, said the lawyer, appeals courts had held such instructions invalid and the decisions had been reversed.

Finally, Kearns declared, "The sentence of seven years in every event violates the Constitution of Ohio." He couldn't believe that in passing the obscenity law the Ohio legislature had intended a woman like Dollree Mapp "should be sent to the penitentiary for seven years for failure to destroy the articles of her roomer, which it was expected were to be called for." If so, he added, "that law would be unconstitutional."

He referred to a decision from the Supreme Court of the United States which he felt supported his claim, and he added a couple of state court decisions that upheld his point. In one, a local ordinance (law) in New Jersey required that a license be obtained to own a gum vending machine. The penalty for violation was set at $24,600 fine or thirty years in jail. The law, reported Kearns, was held unconstitutional under the constitutions of both New Jersey and the United States. (In the federal constitution, the Eighth Amendment, part of the Bill of Rights, forbids "cruel and unusual punishment.")

The severe penalty of the Ohio obscenity law, as applied to Dollree Mapp with a seven-year sentence, argued her attorney, made the law unconstitutional and thus the judgment against her should be overturned by the appeals judges.

Of course, these arguments were opposed by the state's prosecuting attorney, Gertrude Mahon, who denied that the lower court had erred or that the Ohio law was unconstitutional. The appeals judges accepted her version and on March 28, 1959, turned down the Mapp appeal, directing the Court of Common Pleas to send the convicted woman to jail in keeping with Judge Lybarger's sentence. "Upon review of the entire case," wrote the court's presiding judge, "we find no error prejudicial to the rights of the defendant. The question of punishment is within the exclusive jurisdiction of the trial court, the judgment of the Court of Common Pleas is therefore affirmed."

Once more Kearns made arrangements for still another appeal and for keeping his client free under bail in the meantime. He soon took the Mapp case to the Supreme Court of Ohio, the state's highest court, which sat in the state capital at Columbus. Seven judges made up this panel under Chief Justice Carl V. Weggandt.

As before, Kearns, in brief form, compiled his argument stating why the judgment against Dollree Mapp should be reversed. The papers were filed with the Ohio high court in late May 1959. A couple of weeks later Ms. Mahon filed the state's brief opposing reversal of the judgment.

In this legal round, which everyone assumed would surely settle the case for all time, Ms. Mapp's attorney entered his previous arguments, but expanded upon them by raising questions related to the Constitution of the United States. He did so by claiming that, contrary to the Fourteenth Amendment, the state of Ohio was depriving Ms. Mapp "of life, liberty, or property, without due process of law." Specifically, she was being deprived of those rights provided by:

—the Fourth Amendment because she was convicted with evidence illegally obtained without a warrant,

—the Eighth Amendment because seven years for such an offense was "cruel and unusual punishment."

The State Supreme Court moved slowly and deliberately and months went by without any evident activity. That fall, nearly five months after the appeal was initiated, Kearns and his client were surprised to learn one day that they were about to be supported by the Ohio Civil Liberties Union, a state chapter of the American Civil Liberties Union, a national organization established many years earlier to help people protect their civil liberties. On October 24, 1959, the organization asked permission to file a brief *amicus curiae* (Latin for "friend of the court"). The court allowed the action and the Union's statement, when filed, supported and expanded upon Kearns' contention that the Ohio obscenity law was unconstitutional.

Nothing happened throughout the winter. Dollree Mapp worried as usual, but now, nearly two years after sentencing, her fear of prison had become such a way of life that she could hardly remember anything different. She frequently telephoned Kearns, but he couldn't tell her anything new. He could only counsel patience. However, he was hopeful, for he felt that in this highest of all Ohio courts, Ms. Mapp would receive the best hearing to date on the several issues he and the Ohio Civil Liberties Union had placed before the seven judges.

On March 23, 1960, their decision was handed down. Dollree Mapp lost. But she lost in a way that would have left her a winner in most forums. Four of the seven judges, a majority, voted to reverse the lower court decision because the obscenity law was unconstitutional; however, she needed six votes to make it so. The rule for this was found in the Constitution of Ohio, a part of Section 2, Article IV, which read:

"No law shall be held unconstitutional and void by the Supreme Court without the concurrence of at least all but one of the [seven] judges. . . ."

The three judges who voted to uphold the judgment against Dollree Mapp admitted that it depended on illegally seized evidence. "There is, in the record," stated the three judges, in the opinion of the court, "considerable doubt as to whether there even was any warrant for the search of the defendant's home. No warrant was offered in evidence, there was no testimony as to who issued any warrant or as to what any warrant contained, and the absence from evidence of any such warrant is not explained or otherwise accounted for in the record."

The opinion went on to say that Ohio law "requires a search warrant to 'particularly describe the things to be

102

searched for'." But then it confessed, "Admittedly . . . there was no warrant authorizing a search of defendant's home for any obscene materials.

"However," the opinion writer added hastily, "this court has held the evidence obtained by an unlawful search and seizure is admissible [as evidence] in a criminal prosecution." Furthermore, the statement pointed out that the Supreme Court of the United States "does not usually prevent a state court" from using illegally obtained evidence. *Wolf v. Colorado* was cited in support.

So, without legal reason to act otherwise, the three judges voted to affirm the decision of the lower courts in the Mapp case. Three votes were enough to control the outcome.

A dissent to the court's decision, written by Judge Herbert, explained why a majority of the judges had voted to reverse Ms. Mapp's conviction. While the writer felt obscene literature was possibly harmful to the immature mind, he could not agree that mere private possession of such literature by an adult should constitute a crime. He continued:

The right of the individual to read, to believe or disbelieve, and to think without governmental supervision is one of our basic liberties, but to dictate to the mature adult what books he may have in his own private library seems to the writer to be a clear infringement of his constitutional rights as an individual. Does the state have the power to prohibit the possession of chemistry books because from such books one might learn how to make a bomb or poisonous gas? Is the

103

possession of medical books by a layman to be
blamed because of the possibility that he might
learn about abortion and perhaps put such
knowledge to use?

Because of this fundamental right to privacy, Judge
Herbert continued, "we certainly should scan carefully
the method by which the evidence was acquired for
[the Mapp] conviction." He explained:

I would hold no brief for the defendant here if the
evidence had disclosed a commercial purpose in
the possession of these books. Had there been
found printing presses with evidence of their
criminal use or a sufficient volume of books to
indicate the purpose of distribution, commercial
or otherwise, we might hold that the privacy and
constitutional immunity of defendant's home from
unlawful search and seizure had been lost by her
own conduct . . . but on the undisputed facts, as
disclosed in this record, I can not so conclude.

The dissenter lamented that despite his strong
feelings on the unconstitutionality of the obscenity law
"a bare majority of this court is powerless to invalidate"
the law.

A few days after the Ohio Supreme Court's decision
was announced, Al Kearns applied to the same court for
a rehearing of the case. Nine days later his motion was
denied. The attorney then asked the court for a "stay of
execution," an order allowing Ms. Mapp to remain free
on bail while further appeals were considered and
possibly initiated. It was granted.

In the next few weeks Kearns, consulting Dollree Mapp and involving his young partner, Walter Greene, decided to appeal. The majority vote by four of the seven Supreme Court judges was highly encouraging despite its failure to win. And the majority's dissenting opinion focused favorably on the very issues that would count in the next step of the appeals process, for they were issues grounded in the Constitution of the United States.

The next move, as always, was upward, but for Kearns, who had never taken the step before, it was a big one. It led directly to the Supreme Court of the United States. He assigned Greene to the job of getting them there.

9

Cherry Blossoms and Eleven Printed Lines

In the afternoon of March 28, 1961, Dollree Mapp and a friend, Florence Keys, arrived in Washington, D.C., after a long drive from Cleveland. As they had proceeded across the Appalachians, spring, newly arrived, had beautified the countryside to the extent of often causing Ms. Mapp to forget the purpose of the journey, that it was leading her to the nation's "court of last resort." Her case had been accepted there and was scheduled the next day for "oral arguments," when the attorneys for both sides would actually speak before the Court. This appeal was the last of her chances to avoid the seven-year jail sentence that had unsettled her mind day and night for nearly three years.

In Washington the two women checked into a motel which, they had been told, would accept black people. In 1961 the segregation of blacks from whites, openly or implied, was still an unhappy fact of life in the nation's capital. The motel was in a poorer section of the city which, oddly enough, was only a few blocks from the Capitol and the nearby home of the Supreme Court of the United States.

Soon after the two women had checked in, they left the motel for a walk to the Supreme Court Building, which neither had ever seen before. The city around Capitol Hill, the site of the Court, was stunningly beautiful. The day was unusually warm and sunny, and the city's renowned cherry blossoms were in full bloom. Schoolchildren on their annual springtime pilgrimages were everywhere. In a few minutes Dollree Mapp and her friend caught sight of the Supreme Court Building, which stands like an ancient palace across the Capitol Plaza opposite the Senate wing of the Capitol. The great marble structure was startlingly white in the afternoon sun.

As they came up to the Court, they crossed the sweeping white marble plaza leading to the magnificent, ornate building with its virtual hillside of wide marble steps ascending to the high, colonnaded portico. Across the frieze atop the portico were the words "Equal Justice Under Law," and above the inscription were nine sculptured figures of men in robes, the center one representing "Liberty Enthroned."

Dollree Mapp had a camera, and she took some snapshots of the imposing building, so brilliantly illuminated by the sun. She and her friend then ascended the broad steps toward the front doors, which are sliding bronze panels with eight relief pictures illustrating the evolution of justice from early Greece and Rome to modern times. Passing through the mammoth columns of the portico, the two visitors entered through the doors into the Court's large Main Hall, bordered by massive marble columns. The huge hall was quiet, and except for a few uniformed guards and a scattering of tourists the vast space was empty.

Ms. Mapp spoke with one of the guards, a young black man, who politely answered her questions about the Court. In a few minutes he was surprised when the woman revealed she was an appellant whose case, *Mapp v. Ohio*, was scheduled for oral arguments the next day. Learning this, he became more open, as if the two women had suddenly become part of the great institution, and he walked them around to provide a more detailed look at the building. That evening he dropped by the motel and had dinner with the visitors. He promised to watch for them the next day and make certain they would have good seats in the main courtroom. They should come there early, well before noon, he said.

The next morning Dollree Mapp and her friend had breakfast, and after some minor sightseeing at the Capitol building, they went to the Supreme Court. The young guard had made arrangements for them to sit in the courtroom before any activity had begun. The famous room with twenty marble columns was backed by deep red drapes and set off with wooden trim and furnishings of dark, rich mahogany. It was terribly silent as Ms. Mapp and her friend sat there waiting for the Court to convene.

"I got such good vibrations from being there," she said later. "It made me feel good. Being raised in a modest family, it made me feel important to be in the Court and to think they would be talking about me."

Dollree Mapp was there specifically because of certain legal steps that had been taken soon after she had lost in the Supreme Court of Ohio. And she was there because the justices of the Supreme Court of the

United States were interested in the issues that her case raised. While she was intensely concerned with staying out of jail, they were concerned with the long-range constitutional implications of the law and official procedures that would send her to prison.

Soon after the Supreme Court of Ohio had upheld the decisions of the lower state courts, Walter Greene, at Al Kearns' request, filed with the Ohio court a Notice of Appeal to the Supreme Court of the United States. It asked the clerk of Ohio's highest court to send a transcript of the Mapp case to Washington to the clerk of the nation's highest court. The notice included eight questions that would be presented in an appeal to the High Court. All but one concerned the Constitution of the United States.

Greene, who was now doing a great deal of the legal work on the Mapp case, immediately began writing what amounted to a request for the Supreme Court to accept an appeal from Dollree Mapp. It was called a "Jurisdictional Statement."

While a great many cases are presented to the Supreme Court, only a very small percentage are actually accepted. The great court of last resort reserves itself for only the most fundamental issues related to the highest law of the land, the Constitution, and other legal matters considered of great significance. Therefore, under federal law the Supreme Court has legal methods of picking and choosing its cases.

There is, however, one kind of situation that legally forces the Court to consider a question. The Court must accept an appeal if:

(1) the appellant lost in the highest court of a state, and

(2) the state court upheld a state law that could be "repugnant" (contrary) to the Constitution of the United States.

The Jurisdictional Statement prepared by Greene was designed to demonstrate that the Ohio obscenity law and its use to indict and convict Dollree Mapp were contrary to the Constitution. He included the story of the case, from when the police came to the Mapp home in 1957 to when she lost in the Supreme Court of Ohio. Then he explained how the facts posed a number of questions as to constitutionality, such as whether or not the police raid violated the Fourth Amendment, and the seven-year sentence violated the Eighth Amendment.

Soon thereafter the state prosecutors, John T. Corrigan and Gertrude Bauer Mahon, filed a "Motion to Dismiss or Affirm" with the High Court in Washington. They explained the facts of the case as they saw them and then argued to dismiss the appeal because there was nothing unconstitutional about the case. They claimed that it had been settled properly and completely within the rights of the state.

" . . . the police powers of a state," they said, "cannot be effectively exercised to eradicate obscenity without legislation such as provided for in the Ohio obscenity statute." The law, they continued, was entirely correct in attempting to wipe out obscene materials from the state, even down to the point of making it illegal for a private individual merely to possess obscene items.

In short, the prosecutors were saying in a very

legalistic, polite style that the Supreme Court had no business involving itself in the Mapp case. It was not in the High Court's jurisdiction (legal authority) to take the appeal.

The justices disagreed, and on October 24, 1960, they issued an "Order Noting Probable Jurisdiction." It was the Court's way of saying "Yes, from what we see we do have jurisdiction, and you, Dollree Mapp, may bring your appeal."

Next came the briefs of both sides, once more debating on paper the two sides of the case. The Mapp attorneys now sent the Supreme Court what was called a "Brief of Appellant on the Merits." In some twenty-seven printed pages Kearns and Greene again explained the case and the contention that their client was being denied her constitutional rights by the Ohio law and the officers of the law. The prosecuting attorneys offered fourteen pages of material defending the state's right to put Ms. Mapp in jail without interference from the federal government. While the Mapp side called on the High Court to reverse the state's decision and thereby set Dollree Mapp free, the state's side urged the justices to affirm what the Ohio courts had done.

As these briefs were being prepared and filed, another important move was under way in Cleveland in favor of Dollree Mapp. The Ohio Civil Liberties Union, which had already been involved in the Ohio Supreme Court (as *amicus curiae*, friend of the court), became more interested in the case than ever, so much so that the Ohio chapter's parent organization, the American Civil Liberties Union, lent its name to the effort. The dissenting opinion that had come with the

112

unusual four-to-three vote of the seven judges had excited the Union's lawyers. The dissent would have held the state's obscenity law to be unconstitutional, which these attorneys firmly believed was correct. This view, they felt, would attract concern at the Supreme Court of the United States, so they decided to remain involved as the case went to Washington.

Their interest illustrated why the *amicus curiae* role is important in our system of justice. The other lawyers in the case, for and against Dollree Mapp, were intent on either setting her free or sending her to jail. The Civil Liberties Union's interest, however, was confined to the constitutional principles of the case. Its lawyers would, therefore, be arguing for the civil liberties of all people, not just one convicted woman.

The Ohio Union's Board of Directors appointed a committee of four lawyers to take on the project. All were volunteers, but highly skilled practitioners of the law, whose deep commitment to civil liberties led them to work without legal fees. The group consisted of Bernard A. Berkman, Fred J. Livingstone, Julien C. Renswick, and David R. Hertz. They usually held their meetings over lunch at the City Club in Cleveland, and at one of the first gatherings they decided that Berkman would carry the main work load on the case.

Bernard Berkman, who was thirty years old, had been in the practice of law only five years. In his law school days he had become intensely interested in constitutional law, but as a young Cleveland attorney he had little chance to take on anything but routine cases involved with state and local law. So to satisfy his broader interest in the nation's Constitution, he had immediately volunteered his services to the Ohio Civil

Liberties Union. Here attorneys could often represent people in defense of their rights under the federal Constitution.

The Mapp case clearly involved a constitutional law, and young Berkman welcomed the opportunity to handle it for his colleagues. He began by reading everything he could about the case and the questions of law it raised. He concluded that it offered two winning lines of argument.

The first had already been well formulated by the Civil Liberties Union. It held that the mere possession of obscene literature could not be a crime, and any law that said so was contrary to the Constitution of the United States. This contention, of course, would apply to the case of Dollree Mapp with her seven-year sentence for mere possession of obscene materials.

Second, Berkman felt that her case also presented a search and seizure issue that could possibly interest the Supreme Court in finally applying the exclusionary rule to the states. This idea was pretty big thinking for the young attorney because it meant suggesting that the High Court overrule *Wolf v. Colorado*, handed down only eleven years earlier.

When Berkman discussed the case with his committee, the other three members were solidly behind the first line of argument attacking the constitutionality of the Ohio law, but they opposed the second line of argument asking the Court to overrule the *Wolf* decision. They didn't say so outright, but they undoubtedly felt the idea was a naive approach, a mark of legal inexperience. Such a reversal, they counseled, would be very unlikely. The Supreme Court does not ordinarily overrule its own work quickly or lightly, they said. It lives by *"stare decisis"* (standing by decisions previously made). The issue of the exclusionary rule as decided in 1949 by the Wolf case was by no means a lightweight matter. Moreover, the man who wrote the *Wolf* opinion for the Court, Justice Felix Frankfurter, was still there, and so were others who had supported him in that case. The justice, known as a staunch fighter for judicial principles, would not give up the *Wolf* decision easily, and that would be formidable opposition.

But young Berkman was determined—or perhaps naive, starry-eyed, whatever—and, while he agreed to attack the constitutionality of the Ohio law, he relentlessly insisted on including an attack on the *Wolf* decision by asking the Supreme Court to overrule and apply the exclusionary rule to the states.

As the Civil Liberties Union brief was finally written, Berkman's desire was realized, but barely so. The brief, when completed, had twenty-one printed pages. Over twenty pages were devoted to a long, involved argument attacking the obscenity law as offending the basic constitutional liberty to read whatever a person desires, and that its use, as in the Mapp case, amounted to unnecessary interference with an individual's right to privacy protected by the Constitution. Only eleven lonely lines on page 20 were finally agreed upon by the committee to satisfy young Berkman's urge to go after the *Wolf* decision. "I was allowed that," he explained, "only because I was doing the bulk of the work." The paragraph read as follows:

This case presents the issue of whether evidence obtained in an illegal search and seizure can constitutionally be used in a State criminal proceeding. We are aware of the view this Court has taken on this issue in *Wolf v. Colorado*, 338 U.S. 25 [the legal reference]. It is our purpose by this paragraph to respectfully request that this Court re-examine this issue and conclude that the ordered liberty concept guaranteed to persons by the due process clause of the Fourteenth Amendment necessarily requires that evidence illegally obtained in violation thereof, not be admissible in state criminal proceedings.

These three sentences were to become one of the most unusual and important paragraphs in the nation's constitutional history. The paragraph was filed along with the other twenty pages with the clerk of the Supreme Court, and so the brief of the *amici* became part of the case.

While older attorneys of the Civil Liberties Union looked at the short, polite attack on *Wolf* and feared it could be an affront to Justice Frankfurter and others on the Court, their eyebrows really jumped when they learned of another Berkman-inspired request of the Supreme Court.

One day the young attorney had called Al Kearns, who had already agreed to the involvement of the Civil Liberties Union in the case, and had asked if he could share the oral argument time before the Supreme Court. Each side, according to a Court rule, would be allotted only thirty minutes to present its case. Kearns had readily agreed that Berkman could take half the time, providing the justices agreed. The young attorney, using Civil Liberties Union stationery, had then written and mailed a routine sort of letter to the Court, asking permission to address the justices with Kearns.

When some of Berkman's older colleagues learned of this, they were appalled. No attorney representing an *amicus* party ever addressed the Court. It simply wasn't done. The justices would see such a request as the work of a true neophyte. It never should have been made.

But while they were worrying over the unthinkable move, a routine kind of reply arrived from the Court. Yes, you may join in the oral arguments, it said. Berkman, expecting a scolding instead of an acceptance, was, of course, elated, and his attorney friends were astonished. It was the first time in history that an *amicus* was given such an opportunity. Why hadn't it been done before? No one like Berkman, ignorant of custom and false assumptions, had ever asked. Since then it has happened numerous times.

Berkman went to Washington on Monday, March 27, 1961, and unlike others visiting the beautiful city he hardly noticed the cherry blossoms. He thought only of the Supreme Court. Few attorneys ever have a chance to appear before the great tribunal, and most are older, experienced practitioners. To have the opportunity to appear on a key constitutional issue at age thirty with only five years in law practice was overwhelming. To Berkman the Supreme Court was the most important, august body in the land—indeed, in the world. To be able to perform there at this early stage of his career was an opportunity he'd never imagined possible.

Berkman arrived in Washington two days before the scheduled hearing so he could observe the Court in action and get a feeling for it. He also wanted to meet with Kearns, who had gone to Washington early. Several times Berkman had tried to get together in Cleveland with the older attorney to coordinate their arguments, but Kearns had always been too busy. Now, in Washington, the Civil Liberties Union lawyer couldn't find Kearns at all. They never even spoke with one another until they arrived in the courtroom and met in a section of seats reserved for attorneys in front of the public seats. Then there was hardly time for a brief hello and an introduction of Berkman to Walter Greene, who was there to assist Kearns. The three men started to talk but were interrupted by the arrival of their opposition counsel, Gertrude Mahon. By the time they were done with greeting her and settling back to business, Berkman recognized that a meaningful conference with Kearns was impossible.

The lawyer for the Civil Liberties Union had never seen Dollree Mapp, nor did he know if she was among the growing number of observers now filing into the huge courtroom. Kearns, if he knew she was present, didn't point her out. At the same time, as Ms. Mapp and her friend quietly observed the gathering lawyers from their seats in the public section, she had no idea that Berkman was there to represent her. Kearns had failed to tell her about the Civil Liberties Union's part in the case. The idea of *amicus curiae* was completely foreign to her.

As the hour of noon approached, the courtroom was filled with visitors, members of the press, attorneys, and officials of the High Court. At exactly 12:00, silence suddenly settled over the room in anticipation of what was about to happen. An elegantly dressed man walked

118

out from among the tall drapes and marble columns behind the long mahogany bench where the justices would sit. He was the marshal of the Supreme Court. He stopped by a small desk at the right side of the bench, bowed to the people present, and then stood stiffly at attention. In a moment another man who was already seated at an adjacent desk stood and rapped a gavel. He was the Court's crier, and he announced:

"The honorable, the chief justice and associate justices of the Supreme Court of the United States!"

With that pronouncement everyone in the room stood as nine men in black robes walked quickly from behind the velvet drapes and moved to their respective chairs behind the bench. The center chair was taken by Chief Justice Earl Warren. Four associate justices sat on each side of him, with the most senior members closest to him on either side.

"Oyez, Oyez, Oyez!" called out the crier, repeating the old French word for "hear ye." "All persons having business before the honorable, the Supreme Court of the United States, are admonished to draw near and give their attention, for the court is now sitting. God save the United States and this honorable Court!"

The justices for a minute or so arranged papers on the bench before them and leaned to one side or another to converse. Here sat what was to become known, famously and infamously, as the Warren Court. It was a mixture of appointees whose tenures on the high bench extended back as far as 1937 and as recent as 1958, with three Presidents having made the appointments.

On each side of Chief Justice Earl Warren, who had been appointed by President Dwight D. Eisenhower, were appointees of President Franklin D.

Roosevelt—Hugo L. Black (appointed in 1937), Felix Frankfurter (1939), and William O. Douglas (1939). One Truman appointee was present, Tom C. Clark. Last, and least in seniority, were four more Eisenhower appointees—John M. Harlan (1955), William J. Brennan, Jr. (1956), Charles E. Whittaker (1957), and Potter Stewart (1958).

After some opening business related to other cases, Chief Justice Warren read aloud from a paper, announcing:

"Case Number 236. Dollree Mapp versus the state of Ohio."

The sound of her name sent a chill through Ms. Mapp. It was unreal to hear one of the nine black-robed men suddenly uttering her name.

When the clerk of the Supreme Court announced that the attorneys were present, the chief justice said, "Mr. Kearns!"

Al Kearns, neatly dressed and carefully groomed, the traditional flower in his lapel, stood up and stepped to the lectern. He was amazingly calm. He smiled at the nine austere, black-robed listeners only a few feet away. By his comportment, one might have thought he was at home in Cleveland in one of his hundreds of appearances before the city's municipal court.

10

The Question
They Didn't Argue

A few minutes after rising to address the Supreme
Court, the Cleveland criminal lawyer collided with one
of the most learned and eloquent, but demanding
justices ever to serve on the highest bench in the land,
Felix Frankfurter. In twenty-two years on the Court,
making him the second most senior justice present, the
former Harvard law professor had earned a reputation
of being hard on nervous lawyers facing the nation's
greatest tribunal often for the first and only time. The
demands and remarks he generally aimed at lawyers
had become known as the "Felix problem."

Felix Frankfurter, who was born in Vienna, Austria,
in 1882 and had come to America with his parents at age
twelve, distinguished himself as a scholar at the City
College of New York and Harvard Law School. Later
he spent twenty-five years teaching law at Harvard, but
his great energy and learning spilled over into many
other areas of law and politics. He was an adviser to
Presidents Wilson and Roosevelt and involved himself
in a variety of national affairs.

He became widely known to the public with a book

on the famous Sacco-Vanzetti case in which Nicola Sacco and Bartolomeo Vanzetti were tried and convicted for murder and robbery at Braintree, Massachusetts. The two men, a shoemaker and a fish peddler, were considered radicals and their trial, which became a national cause with cries for its review, led to their execution. Frankfurter's book sharply questioned that the two men had been justly convicted, and it marked the professor as a great, even radical, civil libertarian. His involvement in other cases heightened this image, and when he was appointed to the Supreme Court in 1939, it was thought he would be a great libertarian leader of other justices, especially in behalf of the Bill of Rights.

Immediately Justice Frankfurter chilled the liberals' assumption with the position he took on two cases brought by a religious sect, the Jehovah's Witnesses, against state laws forcing their children in public schools to salute the flag against their religious convictions. The justice, in the first of the two Flag Salute cases, led a new liberal contingent of the Court, Justices Hugo L. Black, William O. Douglas, and Frank Murphy, in voting against two young Witness children, who had been expelled from school for refusing to salute the flag. The justice felt that the Court, in returning the youngsters to their classrooms, would wrongfully become the school board of the nation. The decision, in a sense, backfired on Justice Frankfurter. His liberal admirers were appalled by the decision, and Justices Black, Douglas, and Murphy soon admitted publicly they had made a mistake in supporting it. The Witnesses won a second case, but Justice Frankfurter stuck to his principles and still voted against them.

As time went on, he became known as a very conservative member of the Court. He was intensely concerned that the Court's judicial role and procedures be precisely defined, strengthened, and adhered to. In regard to the Court's role, he firmly advocated a policy of "judicial restraint" which would strictly limit the Court's great power to issues involving only the most direct and obvious conflicts with the Constitution. He insisted that the Court should be extremely careful to act only as a court and avoid anything that could be seen as being in the province of legislatures. He feared "judicial lawmaking," in which the Court's decision could be viewed as actually making or altering law instead of only weighing and interpreting it. Justice Frankfurter also demanded a rigorous intellectual approach to the technical, procedural side of law in which "the personal notions of judges" had no place. This was illustrated in the Flag Salute cases, in which the justice personally sympathized with the plight of the Witnesses' children, but felt the High Court was simply not in a position to help them. His philosophy had many important contributions for the conduct of the great Court, but in the eyes of many observers, it changed Justice Frankfurter's image from a liberal, deeply concerned for individual rights, to a conservative coldly caught up in technical matters without regard for human concerns.

All this was reflected in the opinion that he wrote for the Court in 1949 for *Wolf v. Colorado*. To force the states to throw out illegally obtained evidence—thus to adopt the exclusionary rule—was in Justice Frankfurter's mind an instance of the Court's making law. He still felt that way the moment Al Kearns stepped to the lectern before the High Court, and it was soon evident, through his questions, that the justice wanted to block any changes in the Court's point of view as set forth by his own hand twelve years earlier in *Wolf v. Colorado.*

But Kearns, with police-court finesse, was more than Justice Frankfurter could take, not because of the lawyer's legal learning, but because of his lack of it.

As the unperturbed Kearns got under way, he was promptly interrupted by Justice Frankfurter. He wanted to know if the attorney felt that *Wolf v. Colorado* should be overruled.

The lawyer nonchalantly said no, he didn't think so, but the manner of his reply betrayed that he probably didn't know much, if anything at all, about the *Wolf* decision. The justice, author of the *Wolf* opinion, was clearly irked, but he let it go and Kearns returned to his prepared argument.

Suddenly he was interrupted again. Once more the famous justice was peering through his pince-nez, lifting up in his chair and leaning forward across the large bench to cast a second question. He wanted to know what Kearns felt about another search and seizure decision handed down in recent years. For the second time Kearns, fully composed, unruffled, finessed an answer that once more revealed he was short on homework. Still the justice, though obviously more irritated than before, sat back.

The third interruption, however, brought a full, classic demonstration of the "Felix problem." The justice asked Kearns, "Do you feel the facts here in the case of Mapp are the same as in *Rochin v. California*?" He was referring to the "stomach pumping case" in which the police ordered Rochin's stomach to be

124

pumped to retrieve evidence he had swallowed. The opinion, also written by Justice Frankfurter, had said that such evidence couldn't be admitted to a trial because it offended the conscience of the Court.

"Your Honor," replied Kearns, "I'm not sure—"

"Mr. Kearns!" interrupted the justice, abruptly, "you have cited *Rochin v. California* in your brief!"

"Yes, sir."

"Have you read *Rochin v. California?*"

"Well, your Honor," said Kearns, pointing to his assistant Walter Greene, "you know I am a very busy man and have to depend on my young assistant here . . ."

But there was no need to continue. Justice Frankfurter had stopped listening. In fact, he whirled his chair nearly a hundred and eighty degrees so that its high, black leather back was all that anyone in front of the bench could see. He had had enough, and there he waited until the Cleveland practitioner had used up his half of the thirty minutes allotted to his side.

In a sense, the fiery justice had met his match, not intellectually but in unflappable comportment. Kearns had been through too many courtroom fracases to let a mere judge, albeit one of the highest in the land, ruffle his flowered lapel. He continued to the end of his prepared statement and then said to the eight justices still listening, "I would like to give the last half of my time to Mr. Bernard Berkman. He's an executive of the Civil Rights Commission."

Young Berkman, who was getting a grip on himself for the greatest experience of his legal life, was astonished. His knees nearly buckled as he rose. "Civil Rights Commission?" he thought as he moved to the lectern. "I've got to correct that. What a horrible way to start."

Once in place, Berkman glanced up at the impressive array of faces staring at him from above the long mahogany bench. There they were, the men he had read so much about, individuals that he revered, making up the most highest Court in the nation. Only one face was missing, for Justice Frankfurter was still turned away from the front, but his chair was beginning to rotate slowly, bringing him back into view.

"I am sorry," Berkman began, "but my colleague misspoke. I am really representing the Ohio Civil Liberties Union, a chapter of the American Civil Liberties Union, not a civil rights commission."

Suddenly, Justice Frankfurter, his chair front and center again, delivered a charge:

"Now!" he admonished, "don't you use this precious time for propaganda purposes for your organization!"

The statement left Berkman reeling. He couldn't understand. Justice Frankfurter before coming to the High Court had been a staunch member of the American Civil Liberties Union—a fact, indeed, that was brought up when he was being confirmed by the United States Senate.

But Berkman, his mouth rapidly going dry, his mind failing to produce an answer, didn't have to reply. To his amazement Chief Justice Warren did it for him in a quiet way. The chief justice, who was actually only a few feet from the speaker's lectern, leaned toward Justice Frankfurter, who held the next chair, and in a low voice, that Berkman barely heard, said, "Oh, cut it out!" The nervous young attorney got under way, though haltingly.

Berkman had a carefully prepared talk but, as he had expected, only a small fraction of it was uttered. Several of the justices used up the attorney's time with questions, each trying to elicit something to support points of view of particular interest. Some caused him to talk about the constitutionality of the Ohio obscenity law. But others probed for considerable time into the search and seizure issue.

He, too, was asked about *Wolf v. Colorado*. Did Kearns really mean the Court should not overrule the decision? Berkman replied that he felt his colleague had actually misunderstood, that, indeed, he meant to say yes, not no. Berkman was also asked by Justice Frankfurter if the Mapp case was like *Rochin v. California*. The young lawyer said no, the events at the Mapp house should not shock the Court's conscience. He said so because he didn't want this case to become simply another exception to the states' failure to impose the exclusionary rule. It might free Dollree Mapp, but it wouldn't change things in general.

When he was through and Gertrude Mahon was having her turn trying to argue that the Court should allow Ohio to do as it pleased with its obscenity law, Berkman realized that through their questions to him the chief justice and several of the associate justices had possibly tipped their hands. They had been more interested in that lonely, single paragraph of his brief than in all the rest of the words. They were evidently taken by his request that the issue behind *Wolf v. Colorado* be reexamined and that they conclude "evidence illegally obtained . . . not be admissible in state criminal proceedings."

Even as Berkman finished, Dollree Mapp was still

not clear as to why he, a total stranger to her, had appeared before the great Court in her behalf. She also clearly felt now that if she were to win, Berkman would be largely responsible.

Gertrude Mahon began her argument with a laugh-provoking apology. She said that one of the four obscene books found in Ms. Mapp's home was missing. It had disappeared while the exhibits were in the Supreme Court of Ohio.

"Was the clerk of that court prosecuted?" asked Justice Potter Stewart, unable to contain himself. Smiles spread along the bench.

"No!" said Ms. Mahon, demurely.

As she proceeded, the justices asked a great deal about the obscenity law. They were obviously amazed at its breadth, that it made it a serious crime simply to possess anything that could be called obscene.

"Mrs. Mahon," said Justice Frankfurter, "suppose that I were a bibliophile. I collect first editions, and I have an obscene book—not for that reason, but because it was printed in 1527."

"Yes?" said the woman prosecutor, carefully following his story.

"Am I guilty?" he said.

"Any collector of obscenity would be guilty," she replied.

"Mark Twain was one of the biggest collectors!" the justice added, smiling. "I can tell you right now where the collection is—but that is outside your jurisdiction."

Ms. Mahon didn't know whether to laugh or remain serious. The incident clearly had a double edge.

Then Justice Frankfurter wanted to know if Ms. Mahon had really investigated the university libraries of Ohio. He was sure that their shelves had porno-graphic literature. They were well known to literary historians, he explained, and added facetiously: "I shan't mention them here lest people run to the bookstores."

"I can't believe that any libraries have material of the kind in this case," Ms. Mahon rejoined. "If they do someone should be prosecuted."

Justice Frankfurter wanted to know what would happen if she caught a psychiatrist using obscene books for some purpose related to mental health. The Ohio prosecutor said she would arrest him.

"Oh, I'm not stimulating you to any prosecutions," Justice Frankfurter said, as if he had gone too far.

When Ms. Mahon was finished, the oral arguments for *Mapp v. Ohio* were over and the principals left the courtroom.

On her way out Dollree Mapp spoke with the young guard who had helped her and her friend get a seat. "I really want to know the minute they decide my case," she said.

"Oh, they'll telegraph your lawyer," the young man explained.

"But will you know when it happens?" she asked.

"Well, I can watch for the decision."

"Will you phone me collect the minute it happens?"

"It will be on a Monday. They always hand down decisions on Mondays."

"Then will you do me a favor? Phone collect every Monday? I won't be able to stand it not knowing. Call me anyhow, whether they decide my case or not—every Monday."

The guard agreed and Monday after Monday he

made a collect call to Dollree Mapp's home in Cleveland. Each Monday she was waiting for the call.

Twelve weeks went by and each Monday's call was always "No decision today!" Ms. Mapp once asked if the caller might somehow find out her fate even before it was announced. The request practically frightened the guard. The Court's secrecy was sacred, he explained, far greater than the army's. He'd never be able to find out.

On Monday, June 19, 1961, Ms. Mapp's phone rang as usual and she rushed to pick it up.

"Reversed!" the young man practically shouted.

Dollree Mapp knew what the term meant but was befuddled. "What, what . . . ?" she muttered.

"You won! Won!"

She broke into tears, as if she had lost. But the seven-year sentence was lifted, suddenly and wonderfully, and finally the woman on Milverton Road could relish the true feeling of freedom in a way that few people had ever experienced. She cried and cried with joy. But, regaining her composure, she soon picked up the telephone and called Al Kearns.

"We won!" she said excitedly when he was put on the wire.

"How do *you* know we won?" he asked, surprised. She explained, and a while later the fact was confirmed by a telegram to Kearns from the Supreme Court.

The news of *Mapp v. Ohio* flashed across the country, and was broadcast and printed widely.

"The Supreme Court overruled today a landmark decision of 1949," said the New York *Times* under a large headline on its lead story of the day, "and held that the Constitution forbids the use of illegally seized evidence in state criminal trials.

"The vote was 5 to 4 for taking the historic step. . . ."

The five votes in favor came from Chief Justice Warren, and Justices Black, Douglas, Brennan, and Clark. Justice Clark wrote the opinion for the Court.

Early in the opinion its author had to get around a difficult problem caused by attorney Kearns' reply to Justice Frankfurter about the *Wolf* decision. The lawyer, it will be recalled, had said he wasn't calling for *Wolf* to be overruled. This meant that the justices had heard no argument from him, the leading attorney, on the very key point of their decision. But in his third footnote of the opinion, Justice Clark pointed out that the *"Amicus Curiae* . . . did urge the Court to overrule Wolf."

This footnote represented an important but delicate matter in the decision. It would seem logical that the justices should not act on such a substantial historic issue unless it was thoroughly argued in front of them. Not only did Kearns reject the idea of overruling *Wolf* when asked about it, his brief to the Court hadn't even mentioned *Wolf*. Indeed, during the oral arguments Kearn left the impression, at least with one observer, that he had never even heard of the Wolf case. So how could the justices act on something that the appellant didn't ask for, didn't, for that matter, even mention?

But a majority of the Court did act, and they leaned hard on Berkman to support their landmark decision. They felt his brief—with his eleven-line paragraph— and his replies during the oral argument were sufficient for what they did. It was an unusual but not completely

131

new twist for the High Court to act this way. The dissent, written by Justice Harlan, joined by Justices Frankfurter and Whittaker, dwelled upon the point.

Justice Harlan noted that with minor exceptions the entire case, as they had read and heard it, was about the constitutionality of Ohio's obscenity law, but then the majority of five justices used the case to decide the historic search and seizure issue which had been, at the most, a side issue. The dissenters found this truly a misuse of judicial power. They saw it as an instance of five members of the Court practically deciding in private—reading no comprehensive briefs nor listening to well-rounded arguments—to overrule a recent decision on a highly important question bearing directly upon criminal proceedings in the states. Justice Harlan felt it was a case in which "our voice becomes only a voice of power, not of reason." The decision, he said, was "bewildering, unfortunate, ill-considered, far-reaching."

Nevertheless the majority did overrule. The five men were obviously ready and waiting to do it. Dollree Mapp appeared conveniently to give them cause, as meager as it might seem, and the states were finally forced to exclude illegally seized evidence from criminal trials. State prosecutors now had to live by the exclusionary rule, as had their federal counterparts for the past forty-six years. In the Court's opinion Justice Clark wrote:

Today we once again examine Wolf's constitutional documentation of the right to privacy free from unreasonable state intrusion, and, after its dozen years on our books, are led by it to close the only courtroom door remaining open to evidence secured by official lawlessness in flagrant abuse of that basic right, reserved to all persons as a specific guarantee against that very same unlawful conduct. We hold that all evidence obtained by searches and seizures in violation of the Constitution is, by the same authority, inadmissible in a state court.

In his conclusion the opinion writer stated:

Our decision, founded on reason and truth, gives to the individual no more than that which the Constitution guarantees him, to the police officer no less than that to which honest law enforcement is entitled, and, to the courts, that judicial integrity so necessary in the true administration of justice.

At long last, the protection of the Fourth Amendment had been given to all the people by their court of last resort. *All* officials of the law were now compelled to abide by the highest law of the land to conduct searches and seizures only if reasonable and with a warrant issued by a judge "upon probable cause . . . and particularly describing the place to be searched, and the persons or things to be seized."

The decision hit hardest at the twenty-four states which, under their own laws, still admitted illegally seized evidence in criminal trials. The other twenty-six had adopted the exclusionary rule. As the implications of the decision settled into their thinking, police in many areas questioned its wisdom. Law enforcement officials who had ignored the use of search warrants during their entire careers now saw the Fourth Amendment, with its requirement that investigators leave their hot trails of evidence to obtain court-approved warrants, as a shackle preventing the efficient, effective apprehension of criminals.

"Devastating!" said Sergeant Carl Delau, who, upon hearing about the decision, suddenly felt he had unleashed a monster upon his police colleagues. "If the Court threw the case out on the basis of illegal search and seizure, if they're going to be that technical, that ties our hands in law enforcement."

In Cleveland, where Dollree Mapp's name had received scant attention in newspapers in the 1950s, there was surprise. "No one would have dreamed it," said a Cleveland *Press* editorial, "but a filthy book and picture case originating in Cleveland in 1957 has just resulted in a decision by the U.S. Supreme Court that will influence law enforcement all over the country. . . . With good reason, the 5 to 4 ruling is regarded as the most drastic limitation ever imposed on state criminal procedure in a single move."

Mapp v. Ohio, with the nation's police often its antagonist, was to become one of the most controversial decisions ever handed down by the Supreme Court. But while officers of the law were champing over the abrupt tightening of their bits, many of the defenders of civil liberties had the words of Justice Louis Brandeis running through their minds, that "Decency, security and liberty alike demand that government officials shall be subjected to the same rules of conduct that are commands to the citizen . . . [that when] the government becomes a lawbreaker, it breeds contempt for law. . . ." He concluded, "Against that pernicious doctrine this Court must set its face."

While the name *Mapp* met with disdain from many of those who were restrained by it, to others it symbolized the kind of law and order that Justice Brandeis envisioned. A small tribute to his concept is found in a colorful booklet available for visitors at the Supreme Court Building—*Equal Justice Under Law, The Supreme Court in American Life*. It declares:

"Dollree Mapp may stand for anyone who thinks a government should obey its own laws."

Epilogue

A few months less than nine years after winning her landmark decision before the Supreme Court of the United States, Dollree Mapp was again the subject of a search and seizure by police. Having moved from Cleveland, she now ran a used-furniture store in the section of New York City known as Harlem. She lived several miles away in yet another section of the large city, Jackson Heights, which is in Queens County on Long Island.

On February 18, 1970, detectives from an elite narcotics unit appeared at Ms. Mapp's Jackson Heights home with a search warrant. She let them in, and they began looking for drugs which they suspected she was selling. At that very moment other members of the same police unit were searching the apartment of Alan Lyons in another part of Queens. Lyons, a young black man, was the manager of Dollree Mapp's store. The detectives suspected that the two storekeepers were involved in the illegal possession and sale of heroin.

The officers claimed they had been approached in the previous October by a "confidential informer," a

137

person whom the police had found unreliable in the past. He had said that Lyons and Ms. Mapp were processing and packaging heroin at Lyons' apartment and storing it at her home. A few months later an unnamed detective disguised as a dope addict allegedly bought heroin from Lyons. Then the narcotics officers, continuing to act on tips from their informant, began following Dollree Mapp and Alan Lyons as they entered and left their respective homes in Queens. In February one of the detectives, John Bergerson, claimed to have overheard the two suspects talking as they entered Lyons' apartment building. The officer said the conversation indicated the man and woman were about to process and package heroin.

On the basis of these and other claims Detective Bergerson obtained a search warrant that he and his fellow detectives used on February 18. They found a quantity of heroin at Lyons' apartment, but none at Dollree Mapp's home. The most damaging evidence they could locate on her premises was a rent receipt for the apartment where Lyons lived—and even that was made out to someone other than the two suspects.

Nevertheless Ms. Mapp was arrested along with Lyons and charged with the possession of heroin. The following day they were set free on $10,000 bail pending a trial on the charge of possessing more than 16 ounces of heroin, which was extremely serious because under a new law in the state of New York, conviction would carry a mandatory sentence of life imprisonment.

The local newspaper, the Long Island *Press*, reported the arrest, stating that Dollree Mapp had been charged with possession of nearly a million dollars' worth of heroin. The news story pointed out that the narcotics, some three pounds of heroin, had actually been found at Lyons' apartment, but the paper went on to say that the police "theorized" that Dollree Mapp had been at the man's apartment helping him package the heroin.

The story had more than local interest because the detectives arresting Ms. Mapp pointed out to reporters that they had picked up a notable person, the principal figure in the landmark case of *Mapp v. Ohio*. The detectives claimed to have recognized her identity "at a point not far into the investigation." At the same time the arresting officers were careful to point out that they had search warrants which made their two raids legal.

Dollree Mapp believes that her name—widely known by then to America's policemen—had a lot to do with her arrest. She claims that the detective who arrested her following the search of her home made derogatory remarks about her role in *Mapp v. Ohio*, saying that now she would pay for all the criminals who had gone free as a result of the decision.

Among policemen in America the name *Mapp* was certainly well known—and to many law officers it was an infamous word. In finally forcing all state courts to exclude evidence obtained in violation of the Fourth Amendment, the Mapp decision had roused what Erwin N. Griswold, former solicitor general of the United States, described as a "sleeping giant."

In the decade and a half following the Supreme Court's decision, few other legal subjects occupied as much time in the nation's courts as did a great "torrent" of Fourth Amendment cases. A survey conducted by Griswold revealed that search and seizure court decisions totaled over seven thousand in about fifteen years following *Mapp*. This was an unusually large number for a single category of law.

Most of the cases tested state and local police procedures as they were being forced to change under the *Mapp* decision. A search warrant, surprising as it seemed, was a document practically unknown to the police of many American cities. Four years after the decision the deputy police commissioner of New York declared, "We had to reorganize our thinking, frankly. Before this [the *Mapp* decision] nobody bothered to take out search warrants."

One of the immediate problems came purely from lack of police procedure, training, and experience for obtaining legal search warrants. Suddenly faced with such a requirement, policemen often fumbled and lost valuable time while criminals escaped with evidence that might have been found and used against them had a sudden search and seizure been possible.

Soon after the *Mapp* decision attorney Bernard Berkman learned of how two Cleveland policemen heading out for a search one day suddenly remembered they needed a warrant, stopped their patrol car, and asked each other what to do next. They turned around and raced back to their station, but no one there could find a proper form for a search warrant. By the time one was obtained elsewhere, laboriously filled out by the inexperienced policemen and taken to a court for a judge's signature, the officers were certain that the subject of their intended search had long gone.

With this sort of thing happening in city after city, policemen, often failing to acknowledge their own constitutional responsibilities, blamed the *Mapp* decision and the judges who were bound to enforce it. Certainly, many police departments corrected their deficiencies, but others complained of how legal red tape amounted to shackles that delayed policemen while criminals got away.

Of the thousands of search and seizure cases in the nation's lower courts since the *Mapp* decision an unusually high percentage went up to the Supreme Court of the United States. For example, in its October 1972 term (which ended in June 1973) the Supreme Court handed down ten search and seizure decisions. In that term's *United States Reports* (the official publication of the Court's decisions) the ten cases occupied 260 printed pages, about 13 percent of the pages for all cases.

A look at what the Supreme Court has been considering in this area since the *Mapp* decision reveals that the justices have been entangled in a frustrating legal thicket of facts associated with various search and seizure cases. While each decision has arrived at a conclusion for the given set of facts, hardly any have provided broad precedents to guide lower courts in all Fourth Amendment cases. Through these cases the facts of the searches and seizures usually led the justices to consider questions about a few key words of the Amendment. What did the framers of the Constitution mean by "unreasonable searches and seizures"? What did they mean by the need for "probable cause" to issue a search warrant? How specific did they expect a warrant to be in "particularly describing the place to be searched, and the persons or things to be seized"?

Such questions are often perplexing. They are frequently involved with applying basic concepts

141

worked out more than two centuries ago to the complicated world of today. When the Fourth Amendment was adopted, the facts of all searches and seizures had to be relatively simple. They were pretty much limited to homes, commercial buildings, and sailing vessels. Official searchers, customs officers and an occasional constable, were few in number and not well organized. For example, in Philadelphia, when the Constitution was signed, the city didn't have a single policeman. The seizures provided for by the Fourth Amendment were also limited, usually to smuggled or stolen goods.

The facts of today's searches and seizures, of course, are tremendously changed. Police, in highly organized units with the most modern transportation and electronic communication equipment, are found everywhere. They can implement complicated scientific and technical methods in searching for evidence. Their seizures can be something that could hardly have been imagined by the authors of the Fourth Amendment.

A case in point was decided before the Supreme Court in 1973. The facts in the case were these: A man came to a police station one day with his attorney to report that he had found his wife strangled to death. While the husband was at the station a policeman noticed a dark spot on one of the man's fingernails. The officers asked if they might take a scraping from the fingernail to have it analyzed. The man refused, but then, under protest, he was forced to allow the policemen to scrape the nail. Analysis of the minute scrapings revealed the material contained blood cells and bits of skin of the dead woman and fabric from the

142

dead woman's nightgown. The husband was accused of murder.

After a state court allowed the evidence to be used and the husband was convicted of murder, he appealed, contending that in scraping his fingernail without a search warrant the police had conducted an illegal search and seizure under the Fourth Amendment. He won in a federal court, but when the case was appealed to the Supreme Court, he lost. The majority of the justices felt that under the circumstances the unusual search was justified. Otherwise, the stain, once recognized, might have vanished had the husband been allowed even a few seconds by himself. Justice William O. Douglas dissented in the belief that even in these bizarre circumstances the Fourth Amendment should have held against the search.

Such questions, involved with the extremely mobile, highly sophisticated society of this century, have constantly perplexed police, prosecutors, lawyers, judges and Supreme Court justices since the *Mapp* decision declared that illegally seized evidence must be excluded from trials.

What about a policeman who routinely stops a car for a simple traffic violation and then for some good reason strongly suspects it contains stolen goods? Should he go after a search warrant, hoping to find both the car and the goods later? Or should he immediately conduct a search? Would that be "unreasonable"? Under certain emergency circumstances it would not be, according to decisions of the High Court in recent years.

If a policeman is arresting a person caught in the act of burglary, would it be unreasonable to search him for weapons or stolen goods? The Supreme Court has held in a number of cases that a search associated with an arrest is reasonable.

Since the hijacking of airliners became serious, all air travelers must submit to a visual or electronic search of their luggage and persons before boarding a commercial plane. Is each of these thousands of daily searches unreasonable? Some travelers have insisted that their Fourth Amendment rights are being violated. While a number of cases involving such searches have appeared in the nation's lower courts, none as yet has been decided by the Supreme Court.

When *Mapp* was handed down by the Court in 1961, many people believed that the decision finally turned the Fourth Amendment into the strong legal measure its authors had intended to protect individuals from unreasonable searches and seizures. The decision—by rejecting illegally seized evidence for use in courts—would supposedly deter public officials from conducting unreasonable searches and seizures.

But since that time—with philosophical changes on the High Court, with law officers finding ways to get around the *Mapp* ruling, and with official lawlessness condoned in the nation's highest political posts—the Fourth Amendment has not fared well. Warrantless searches are, as always, widely used in the United States.

As Chief Justice Earl Warren and others left the "Warren Court" to be replaced by Chief Justice Warren Burger and appointees selected by President Richard M. Nixon, the Court's philosophy changed, particularly in respect to the Fourth Amendment. The Court's decisions indicated its weight would fall most often on the side of the officer of the law as opposed to the individual citizen. It was particularly evident in that the majority of justices defined fewer and fewer searches as "unreasonable."

By the 1970s the basic idea of the *Mapp* decision seemed to be threatened. The exclusionary rule forced on the states by *Mapp v. Ohio* had a powerful opponent in Chief Justice Burger. He felt that it wasn't justified, that it was simply an escape hatch for "countless guilty criminals." In the mid-1970s the Supreme Court handed down a number of decisions that, one at a time, weakened the exclusionary rule. The majority of justices decided that in certain circumstances illegally seized evidence could be admitted to trials in state courts. For example, in one case the Burger Court decided that it was constitutional for police to make a warrantless search of a glove compartment of an impounded car, although the vehicle was not being held for purposes of an investigation. In another instance, the Court decided it was constitutional for Border Patrol officers to stop cars of their choice and search the vehicles without warrants for evidence that might be used to catch illegal aliens. These and other rulings drew sharp dissents from Justices William J. Brennan, Jr., and Thurgood Marshall, who had been members of the Warren Court. In the Border Patrol decision, handed down in July 1976, Justice Brennan wrote: "Today's decision is the ninth this term marking the continued evisceration of Fourth Amendment protections against unreasonable searches and seizures."

Meanwhile, public officials found that the fruits of illegal searches and seizures could be used in ways other than as evidence in courts. For example, seizures

145

in violation of the Fourth Amendment could be used to force confessions out of individuals who feared the illegally obtained evidence could be used against them. Or the police, without fear of legal retribution, could use searches and seizures purely as harassment of people they might not like—hippielike young people, for example. Unless the Congress of the United States took the unlikely step of passing laws to protect individuals against such practices by providing serious penalties for police offenders, the Fourth Amendment would remain weak.

Disregard and disrespect for the Amendment by the nation's highest officials was revealed over and over in the 1970s. The infamous Watergate burglary of 1972 was essentially a case of illegal search and seizure planned and directed from the White House. Another illegal search and seizure prompted by the White House led burglars to the office of a California psychiatrist who had treated Daniel Ellsberg, the person noted for releasing the Pentagon Papers to the press. Later, Congressional investigations revealed that official lawlessness, clearly in violation of the Fourth Amendment, had been practiced for years by both the FBI and CIA. In search of political information, usually with the excuse of needing it for "national security," the federal agents invaded the privacy of hundreds of American citizens with illegal break-ins, wiretaps, and mail openings. To these agents the priorities established by the nation's founding fathers to guarantee personal privacy had taken a back seat to protecting the immediate decisions of political leaders, as well as the agents' own perception of our national

146

purposes. Their actions against individuals—such as young people opposing the Vietnam War—were precisely the kinds of strong, central government activities feared by the men who framed the Bill of Rights, especially the Fourth Amendment.

It was in this kind of climate, in which "unreasonable searches and seizures" forbidden by the Constitution were officially sponsored and accepted, that Dollree Mapp had her second encounter with the law. After her arrest in 1970 with Alan Lyons for the possession of heroin, she went through two five-week trials in a Queens County court. She lost the first in 1971 and was sentenced to twenty years to life in prison, but on appeal to a higher state court her conviction was overturned and a new trial was ordered. After five more weeks in court Dollree Mapp lost her second trial and was once more sentenced to twenty years to life.

The jury in the second trial deliberated eleven hours. When the guilty verdict was announced, the convicted woman fainted and the courtroom was disrupted by her sister screaming from the spectators' gallery, "There is no justice! There is no justice!" Later, as she stood for sentencing, Dollree Mapp told the judge:

"I am not guilty! God have mercy on your soul!"

The woman who had won the landmark decision which held that "a government should obey its own laws" was sent to a New York State prison for women. Continuing to maintain she was innocent, Ms. Mapp began studying law in prison, determined to regain her freedom. Her family, in turn, provided funds to retain a new attorney, Eleanor Jackson Piel, a person who had proven in other cases that she could be a strong advocate in behalf of the civil liberties spelled out in the Bill of Rights.

In 1975, after other appeals had failed, Dollree Mapp's "petition for *habeas corpus*" (a legal action calling for her release from prison) was heard before the United States Court of Appeals in New York. There Ms. Piel argued that her client's conviction was based on "evidence . . . so slight as to be no evidence at all." As admitted in the trial, the attorney reminded the three federal judges hearing the appeal, "No narcotics were found on the person of Ms. Mapp or at the premises. No evidence was adduced of any narcotics of any kind in her physical possession at any time in these proceedings."

Ms. Piel also went on to attack the search warrant obtained by Detective Bergerson, from a criminal court judge, Joan O'Neill. The lawyer claimed that the document "did not meet the constitutional standards required by the Fourth Amendment." She maintained basically that reasons given to Judge O'Neill did not provide probable cause for issuing the warrant. The information supplied to the judge by Bergerson came from a source proven unreliable in the past, and it had no valid, timely allegations that narcotics would be found in Ms. Mapp's possession.

The three federal judges, practically brushing these arguments aside, denied the petition for *habeas corpus* and Dollree Mapp faced another try at going to the Supreme Court of the United States with a search and seizure case. A petition for certiorari was filed with the High Court in September, 1976, but it was soon denied, meaning that the famous petitioner of 1961 would not be back before the Justices.

Ms. Piel then made one more move that she felt might lead Dollree Mapp to freedom. The attorney went back to the Supreme Court of the State of New York with a motion asking that the Court vacate (declare void) the judgment that led to her client's imprisonment, or at least to grant a new hearing on the matter. In her motion and accompanying documents Ms. Piel argued hard that her client was the victim of a grave injustice and that new evidence would prove it, if only it could be heard. In December, 1976, Justice George J. Balbach denied the motion and it appeared that efforts to free Dollree Mapp were finally at an impassable wall.

Meanwhile, a few close observers of the case can't help but wonder if her plight is not related to her past fame at the Supreme Court—as she claims it is. Specifically, was Detective Bergerson, knowing of Dollree Mapp's past, motivated to punish her for the changes forced upon all police in her name? That was never answered. However, Detective Bergerson's credentials were severely undercut after his arrest of Ms. Mapp. He was prosecuted and found guilty in a New York Police Department trial for illegally accepting $3,500 from a narcotics dealer. He was dismissed from the police force with the loss of his pension. By the time Ms. Mapp's appeal had been denied in the Circuit Court of Appeals, her attorney claimed "Bergerson had been established as a briber, perjurer and an otherwise unreliable member of the Special Investigations Unit."

The fate of Dollree Mapp at the hands of former

149

Detective Bergerson, exercising the power of search and seizure in a way that leaves serious questions unanswered, leads one to think back to the speech of James Otis, which was said to have "breathed into this nation the breath of life" by denouncing the infamous writs of assistance as ". . . a power that places the liberty of every man in the hands of every petty officer." And then one may ask what in truth happened to the liberty of this person who may have stood "for anyone who thinks government should obey its own laws."

Appendix

The two Amendments to the Constitution of the United States involved in the search and seizure cases in this book are:

FOURTH

The right of the people to be secure in their persons, houses, papers, and effects, against unreasonable searches and seizures, shall not be violated, and no Warrants shall issue, but upon probable cause, supported by Oath or affirmation, and particularly describing the place to be searched, and the persons or things to be seized.

FIFTH

No person shall be held to answer for a capital, or otherwise infamous crime, unless on a presentment or indictment of a Grand Jury, except in cases arising in the land or naval forces, or in the Militia, when in actual service in time of War or public danger; nor shall any persons be subject for the same offense to be twice put in jeopardy of life or limb, nor shall be compelled in any criminal case to be a witness against himself, nor be deprived of life, liberty, or property, without due process of law; nor shall private property be taken for public use, without just compensation.

HOW THE *MAPP* CASE
WENT TO THE SUPREME COURT

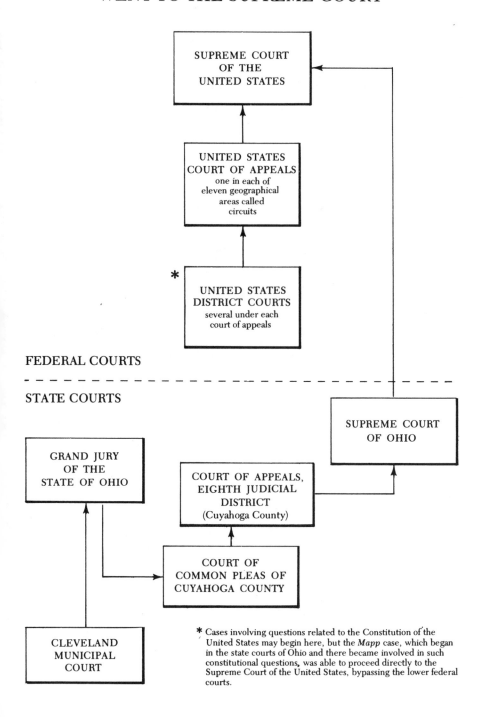

SUPREME COURT
OF THE
UNITED STATES

UNITED STATES
COURT OF APPEALS
one in each of
eleven geographical
areas called
circuits

*

UNITED STATES
DISTRICT COURTS
several under each
court of appeals

FEDERAL COURTS

- -

STATE COURTS

SUPREME COURT
OF OHIO

GRAND JURY
OF THE
STATE OF OHIO

COURT OF APPEALS,
EIGHTH JUDICIAL
DISTRICT
(Cuyahoga County)

COURT OF
COMMON PLEAS OF
CUYAHOGA COUNTY

CLEVELAND
MUNICIPAL
COURT

* Cases involving questions related to the Constitution of the
United States may begin here, but the *Mapp* case, which began
in the state courts of Ohio and there became involved in such
constitutional questions, was able to proceed directly to the
Supreme Court of the United States, bypassing the lower federal
courts.

Major References and Acknowledgments

Adams v. New York. 192 U.S. Reports 585 (1904).

Boyd v. United States. 116 U.S. Reports 616 (1886).

Day, Jack G. and Bernard A. Berkman. "Search and Seizure and the Exclusionary Rule: A Re-Examination in the Wake of Mapp v. Ohio." *Western Reserve Law Review* (December, 1961), p. 56.

Griswold, Erwin N. *Search and Seizure, A Dilemma of the Supreme Court*. Lincoln, Nebraska: University of Nebraska Press, 1975.

Lasson, Nelson B. *The History and Development of the Fourth Amendment to the United States Constitution*. Baltimore: Johns Hopkins Press, 1937.

Mapp v. Ohio. 367 U.S. Reports 643 (1961).

Olmstead v. United States. 277 U.S. Reports 438 (1928) (dissenting opinion).

Rochin v. California. 342 U.S. Reports 165 (1952).

Tudor, William. "The Life of James Otis." Boston, 1828.

Weeks v. United States. 232 U.S. Reports 383 (1914).

Wolf v. Colorado. 338 U.S. Reports 25 (1949).

In addition to the above references and other printed sources, considerable information was brought to this book through personal interviews and by personal assistance received, especially from:

Bernard A. Berkman, attorney, Cleveland, Ohio; Carl Delau, police department, Cleveland, Ohio; Walter Greene, attorney, Cleveland, Ohio; the staff, library, the Cleveland *Press;* the staff, library, the Long Island *Press;* Dollree Mapp, Bedford Hills, New York; Eleanor Jackson Piel, attorney, New York City; and the staff, Yale University Law Library, New Haven, Connecticut.

Index

156

157

Shaker Heights, Ohio, 15, 16
Silverthorne Lumber Co. vs. U. S., 50–51
Stewart, Justice Potter, 120, 128
Supreme Court of the U.S., 9–11, 23, 35, 39, 41, 42–47, 49, 50–56, 60–61, 99–100, 103, 105, 107, 109–10, 114, 117, 118, 122–23, 142, 143, 148–50

Taft, William Howard, 53, 54, 56, 57
Tate, Minerva, 17, 20
Thacher, Oxenbridge, 30
Truman, Harry, 120

United States Court of Appeals, 148–50
United States Reports, 141

Vienna, Austria, 121
Vietnam, 147
Virginia, 32, 33

Warren, Chief Justice Earl, 70, 119, 120, 126, 131, 144
Washington, D. C., 107, 111, 117
Washington, George, 34
Weeks, Fremont, 41, 44
Weeks vs. U. S., 45–47
White, Lieutenant, 88
Whittaker, Justice Charles, 120, 132
Wilson, Woodrow, 121
Wolf, Dr. Julius, 59–67
Wolf vs. Colorado, 61–67, 103, 114–16, 123, 124, 127, 131
Writs of assistance, 29–32
Writs of certiorari, 61